The Quali

THE QUALITATIVE INTERVIEW: ART *AND* SKILL

JEANINE EVERS
FIJGJE DE BOER

eleven
international publishing

Published, sold and distributed by Eleven International Publishing
P.O. Box 85576
2508 CG The Hague
The Netherlands
Tel.: +31 70 33 070 33
Fax: +31 70 33 070 30
e-mail: sales@budh.nl
www.elevenpub.com

Sold and distributed in USA and Canada
International Specialized Book Services
920 NE 58th Avenue, Suite 300
Portland, OR 97213-3786, USA
Tel.: 1-800-944-6190 (toll-free)
Fax: +1 503 280-8832
orders@isbs.com
www.isbs.com

Eleven International Publishing is an imprint of Boom uitgevers Den Haag.

ISBN 978-94-90947-73-6
© 2012 Jeanine Evers & Fijgje de Boer | Eleven international publishing

Printed in The Netherlands

PREFACE

'Interviewing assumes that we can understand the social world by listening to talk and interpreting what is said. Interpersonal skill is involved: we are familiar with the idea that some people are 'good listeners'. Also a skill is being thoughtful about what one has heard. From a researcher's perspective, this means being good at interpretation, drawing on an analytic sensitivity to see the theoretical in the empirical.' (Fielding, 2003:XII)

This book, published in Dutch in 2007 in a different format, describes the theory and practice of qualitative interviewing. One might wonder: why yet another book on qualitative interviewing? In our experience, the art and skill of qualitative interviewing is often underestimated and is seen as being comparable to other types of conversations, whether or not professionally held. Researchers, embarking on a qualitative research endeavour, could use both theoretical knowledge and practical tips and tricks. Existing literature might be divided into literature which stresses techniques, i.e. the Skill, and literature which stresses improvisation and flow, i.e. the Art. Qualitative interviewing then either becomes a trick if one has the appropriate skill, or an empathic conversation which lacks noticing the professional side, being a research question that needs to be answered.

We think both sides are equally relevant to the success of a qualitative interview and, therefore, have tried to deal with both aspects proportionately. Because of the importance of improvising during a qualitative interview, due to its inter-human nature, few concrete examples are described. The interviewer adapts the interview to the person in front of him and responds to what surfaces. We believe, therefore, that too many clues provided through specific examples would be paralyzing instead of enhancing the creativity of the interviewer to go along with what is happening during the interview. He might tend to engage himself with all the clues that were offered in the book and not be totally present in the interview, using all his senses. The boxes are elaborations of a certain topic, they might be disregarded if not deemed necessary.

In Part II of the Dutch version of this book (Evers, 2007) several qualitative researchers were invited to share their experiences with a certain type of qualitative interview or with the adaptation of the interview to certain types of respondents. This part of the book is excluded in the English translation. Furthermore, in the

English version some literature references were added or updated and Chapter 7 has been revised and updated quite extensively as it mostly deals with different types of computer software.

We would like to thank our editor at Boom/Lemma The Hague, Joris Bekkers, for his ongoing belief and support in realizing this project, as well as Paulien Wijnvoord for her assistance in improving our English. The use of 'researcher', 'investigator', 'respondent', 'interviewee' and he/him/his in this book refers to both male and female researchers and respondents.

The Hague, June 2012.

TABLE OF CONTENTS

1 | A SHORT INTRODUCTION TO QUALITATIVE RESEARCH

1.1   WHAT IS QUALITATIVE RESEARCH?

We will start this book on qualitative interviewing with a short introduction about qualitative research because to us, 'qualitative interviewing' is part of a research endeavour; more specifically it is part of a qualitative research project. Therefore, it is important to indicate what we mean by qualitative research.

From the nineties onwards, according to Mulderij (1999:292), qualitative research has been booming. A considerable number of books about the methodology of qualitative research have appeared, often specified for a certain discipline or a specific method. For example, books were published about qualitative research in anthropology (Bryman, 2001; Schensul et al., 1999), nursing science (Holloway & Wheeler, 2002), social sciences (Creswell, 2007; Maso & Smaling, 2004), physical and occupational therapy (Whalley, Hammell, Carpenter & Dyck, 2002), or psychology (Mey & Mruck, 2010). Regarding qualitative research methods, books are divided into subcategories as well, e.g. books on qualitative data analysis (Grbich, 2007, Saldañañ, 2009; Dey, 2005; Boeije, 2010 and Heaton, 2004), on the use of software for analysis (Kelle, 1995; Bazeley, 2007; Friese, 2012), or on interviewing (Rubin & Rubin, 2005; Fielding, 2003; Gorden, 1992 and Bogner, Littig & Menz, 2009). On the other hand, some books offer a general introduction to the methodology of social science research. Here, both qualitative and quantitative research methods are discussed (Bryman, 2004; 't Hartje, Boeije & Hox, 2005). In all of these books qualitative research is discussed and the authors usually adopt their own description of this methodological approach. In the next box, some of these descriptions have been arranged alphabetically by author.

Definitions of qualitative research

To Boeije (2005b:27), the research question in qualitative research aims at topics that can help understand how people give meaning to their social environment and how they act as a result of that. The research methods chosen enable the researcher to describe and – if possible – explain the topic from the perspective of the individuals studied.

According to Bogdan and Knopp Biklen (2007:2), stemming from educational research, qualitative research is an umbrella term for research that has the following features: 'The data collection have been termed *soft*, that is rich in description of people, places, and conversations and not easily handled by statistical procedures. Research questions are not framed by operationalizing variables; rather, they are formulated to investigate topics in all their complexity, in context. While people conducting qualitative research develop focus as they collect data, they do not approach the research with specific questions to answer or hypotheses to test. They also are concerned with understanding behaviour from the informant's own frame of reference. External causes are of secondary importance. They tend to collect their data through sustained contact with people in settings where subjects normally spend their time – classrooms, cafeteria's, teachers' lounges, dormitories, street corners'.

Creswell (2007: 37) describes qualitative research as: 'Qualitative research begins with assumptions, a world view, the possible use of a theoretical lens, and the study of research problems inquiring into the meaning individuals or groups ascribe to a social or human problem. To study this problem, qualitative researchers use an emerging qualitative approach to inquiry, the collection of data in a natural setting sensitive to the people and places under study, and data analysis that is inductive and establishes patterns or themes. The final written report or presentation includes the voices of participants, the reflexivity of the researcher, and a complex description and interpretation of the problem, and it extends the literature or signals a call for action.'
Creswell states that this definition emphasizes qualitative research as a process, starting from philosophical presumptions in which a procedure is determined to investigate the topic. This procedure consists of a certain framework, i.e. a certain research approach and he assumes a research(er) will place himself within a certain movement.

To Maso and Smaling (2004:9-10), qualitative research is a form of empirical research that is characterized by the data collection method, the research design, the kind of analyses done and the role of the researcher. According to them, features of qualitative research are: (a) the data collection is open and flexible, (b) the analysis is done in ordinary language, (c) within the research design, data collection and analysis alternate in a typical cyclical-interactive manner, (d) the research design aims at everyday meaningfulness and the denotation of relationships between phenomena. Thereby, importance is given to all meaning, which is created in interaction between subjects. Finally then, (e) qualitative researchers use themselves as an instrument to gain insight into their subjects' lives.

According to Wester and Peters (2004:16-17), qualitative research is featured by: (a) its orientation on describing the meaning giving of the subjects of research, (b) demonstrating a relationship between accumulated data and concepts, which is an open process resulting from the research, (c) a situation in which the researcher has extended contact with the reality under investigation and the topic under scrutiny allows him to learn about all the aspects of that reality.

From the box above it is obvious that there are several definitions available, each with their own emphasis.

1.2 FEATURES OF QUALITATIVE RESEARCH

If the common elements are deduced from the descriptions in the box above, it is possible to discern six features of qualitative research.

Direct observation in a natural setting
In qualitative research, data are collected in their natural setting. The researcher is interested in the natural environment of respondents and if possible, resides there for longer periods of time. He is in close touch with respondents. There is no resemblance at all with a laboratory situation which is created by the researcher and in which he controls the environment and tries to exclude variables that could influence the research context.

The researcher is pointedly present during data collection
The researcher resides in the field, observes, interviews respondents, determines the length of his stay and the number of interviews, makes a choice of respondents and determines the subject of the interview. The amount of data is not emphasized; the researcher is present in the field to 'learn', to enter a new domain, to understand what is happening there and what is going on. In short, he absorbs all the information from the local environment surrounding him. He can thereby assume the role of the outsider or of the participant. So, the essence is that the researcher travels to the vicinity he would like to investigate in order to learn about it in any way possible.

An inductive procedure usually prevails
The information obtained from the field forms the most important data resource: it is the starting point for the analysis that leads to the final results. The researcher analyzes the data transparently and this leads to a clear overview and interpretation of social reality. He might find a new, and sometimes largely reduced, classification scheme for the data, which is an abstraction of the accumulated information. This could possibly lead to a theory. This then is termed working inductively, which means that the broad information collected in the field, is the groundwork to reach a specific image of the context, with a matching classification or some core category (Coffey & Atkinson, 1996). This working procedure is contrary to the deductive method, in which the researcher departs from an existing theory, derives one or more hypotheses from it, collects the necessary data and verifies if these data can confirm the theory. We do not mean to say that a deductive procedure cannot be used to design qualitative research; compare the framework analysis (Maso & Smaling, 2004). Nevertheless, an inductive approach

is mostly used in qualitative research. Especially during the starting phase of data analysis, the inductive method is used to find concepts that resemble the social reality observed. In the following phases of the analysis newly collected data may be used to verify the formulated concepts. This might be seen as a deductive approach, as the developed conceptual framework will be tested against the newly collected data. This approach is termed constant comparison.

The respondents' perspective is at centre
The aim of the research endeavour is to find and understand how respondents interpret their surroundings and how they act upon their interpretations. Respondents can have different or contrary perspectives, which might be unknown to the researcher. The researcher is interested in this 'inside' world, the private interpretations of the respondent and will, therefore, place his own perspective on matters between brackets while learning about this inside world of the respondent.

Holistic or contextual approach
The researcher is interested in the entire context of the respondent as it occurs while in the field. In a research project concerning illness, for example, this implies the way the illness is experienced with regard to all the aspects of life that it influences. For example, how the illness has changed life for the respondents, what they did before they were ill and how much of that still is possible now, whether their identity has changed as a result of the illness, how their relationship with their partner is now, how they experience being dependent on others and how their perception of the future is.

Results are often in a narrative form
In his reproduction of the respondents' narratives or results from his research, the researcher emphasizes patterns, concepts, themes, meanings, perspectives or strategies of the respondent. Often citations from the interviews are used to underpin his findings. It is not about numbers, percentages, or statistical relations between variables. Instead, the results give a detailed and surveyable image of social reality as it was encountered in the field. For example: respondents are found to have different definitions of 'expensive' when they talk about purchasing something. What they consider 'expensive' is related to how they describe their spending patterns. The researcher tries to relate this finding to a theory or he relates it to other research concerning the same topic. Finally, he tries to relate the significance of the result to the research goal. Let us assume the aim of this fictitious example was to discover what causes people to overestimate their financial position so that they owe more than they could ever pay. In this example, the result described above would be very relevant. Debt counsellors could use the results of this research; they might take this concept of 'expensive' as a starting point for their assistance and discuss specific aspects of spending behaviour with their clients.

Besides these features, qualitative research will mostly be guided by some philo-sophical viewpoint as well which determines the questions asked and the way they are answered. This aspect, which belongs to epistemology or philosophy of science will be dealt with in the next paragraph, which explains some approaches in qualitative research.

1.3   QUALITATIVE APPROACHES: MOVEMENTS AND METHODS

Since the1960s, 'qualitative research' has become an umbrella term for a range of research types that are connected to what Mulderij (1999) also calls movements.[1] He uses the term movements as a common denominator for different perspec-tives from which qualitative research can be done, in other words their epistemo-logical foundation.[2] According to Smaling (1987:247), these perspectives can be traced back to two groups of approaches, the 'paradigmatic' and the 'pragmatic' approach. The **paradigmatic movement**[3] can be subdivided into firstly the **em-pirical-analytic approach**, based on a (neo) positivist view of science, in which reality is objectively recognizable, systematically organized and is considered ver-ifiable and predictable. The second group is the **hermeneutic-interpretative ap-proaches**,[4] which derive from the hermeneutic notion of 'Verstehen'. These ap-proaches originated as resistance to the empirical-analytic ones, because it was felt that especially social reality cannot be known objectively and is not so pre-dictable and systematic. Followers of this movement aimed for greater recogni-tion of the subjective experience of reality and the desire to understand reality from the perspective of the person who experiences it. Thirdly, the **critical**

---

1. A principal solution for this forest of terms has not been found yet. Many terms are being used, such as: approaches, method, movement, strategy or viewpoint, to refer to the procedure and the philosophical background of research. The point is that different backgrounds and sources of in-spiration (have) exist(ed) for qualitative research. For example, the word 'method' is being used in a very philosophical sense, 'the phenomenological method', in a theoretical sense, 'the Marxist method', and in a technical sense, 'the Q-sort method'. The same happens with the term 'techni-que' or 'approach'.
2. Epistemology is defined as the theory of knowledge: what is the essence of knowledge, how is it attained and what are its limits? In short: what reason can we have for a certain conviction or why do we believe in something? (Craig, 2002; Van Dale, 14th edition). In contrast, ontology is the theory of being; it deals with the general properties of things, for example the view that obser-vable reality is independent of human knowledge. (Van Dale, 14th edition, Wikipedia).
3. A paradigm is primarily 'an exemplary, normative example' that indicates which kind of problem has to be investigated and how this should be done. This can only be learned under supervision of experienced persons. In a broader definition by De Vries (1995; 102-103), paradigm stands for: 'the whole of convictions, symbolic generalisations, metaphysical assumptions and values that a rese-archer implicitly adopts by emulating these normative examples'.
4. Examples are: phenomenology, symbolic interactionism, ethnomethodology and ethnography.

approaches,[5] are similar to the interpretive approach in terms of their scientific view but add a political dimension to this, i.e. a social ideal. Therefore, these approaches are sometimes described as emancipatory (Smaling, 1987, 1994; Grbich 2007). The last approach, **constructivism**,[6] is more recent and founded on the assumption that multiple interpretations of reality co-exist and that reality is actively constructed and as such are always 'partial, situated and embodied' (Abma, 1996:18).

Pragmatic approaches do not depart from a theoretical movement to shape their research but use the research question as a guide to methodological and technical choices (Smaling, 1987:265). As such, they might use research methods in a more eclectic manner.

Generally, university-affiliated (PhD-)research is mostly designed according to some paradigm or method. In particular, the hermeneutic-interpretive approaches, the critical approaches and the constructivist approaches can be found here. On the other hand, in applied qualitative research there is generally less space for a paradigmatic approach. This is related to time constraints, costs, and sometimes reluctance to be associated with certain movements. These grounds lead commissioned research to a more pragmatic approach. In some policy circles though, the constructivist approach is booming (Frissen, 1996, Abma, 2002).

Some of these approaches[7] will be considered in the box below. Subsequently, a number of methods that resulted will be discussed in connection to the role of the qualitative interview.

Approaches in qualitative research

Many qualitative approaches are based on an ontological starting point, known from **phenomenology**: the pre-interpreted reality (Bogdan & Biklen Knopp, 2007:24 ff.). Phenomenology is not so much interested in bare facts and causes of the problem, but in the experience and interpretation of the world by people. In tracing that, the researcher puts his experience of the world 'in brackets', i.e. bracketing. He approaches the phenomenon under investigation, i.e. the perception and experience of the respondent, open-mindedly, or at least attempts to do so. 'The' reality does not exist according to the phenomenologist, but is created by people's interpretation of it. The subjective experience and the interpretation thereof by the respondent is the scientific subject, not

---

5. Examples are: feminism, Marxist anthropology and action research.
6. Postmodernism is an example of this.
7. The distinction made between movement, approach and method is historically founded: many methods have emerged from a movement or approach. The grounded theory method is a well-known example and was developed by converting the ideas behind symbolic interactionism to a real research context. Meanwhile, various methods have become more acclaimed than the approach they originated from and sometimes they even were separated from that movement. This, for example, applies to the form of grounded theory, advocated by Strauss and Corbin (oral information by F. Wester).

the factualness of the event. Thus, several interpretations of the same event are possible and can co-exist. This emphasis on the respondents' perspective as a research goal is the essence of all forms of qualitative research. In addition, it is often assumed that besides the respondents' interpretation, there is also a reality that can be observed: what a respondent says during an interview is not 'the truth' but it is a statement, which can be recorded, interpreted, and compared to other statements. The recording method is important to ascertain the authenticity of the statement. Ethnomethodology for example, stems from the phenomenological sociology and the theory of T. Parsons.

Another important approach, **symbolic interactionism**, just like phenomenology, departs from the idea that human experience derives its meaning from the interpretation of it. However, in symbolic interaction the emphasis is on action, in particular interaction with others and their reaction, and how this influences the construction and interpretation of the world. Meaning is negotiable and people construct shared meanings in their interactions. The self, i.e. the own identity, is formulated as well in interaction with the environment (Bogdan & Biklen Knopp, 2007:29). The principles of the grounded theory method are founded on symbolic interactionism.

Ethnomethodology examines the construction of social order through the design and definition of situations by actors. In this context, it is not the actors' perspective that is emphasized, as in phenomenology and symbolic interactionism, but rather the way people handle, develop or change rules in interaction with one another. In short: how people manage to live with each other. For example, the founder Garfinkel investigated this by ordering his students to act differently from the social code in some situation and observed what happened.

Additionally, some (newer) approaches like for instance cultural studies, feminism, postmodernism, institutional ethnography and narrative research are sometimes interpreted as movement. Currently, **feminism**, **critical theory** and **postmodernism** have in common that they believe that there is no 'reality' which can be observed directly. Invisible power issues often determine the interpretation of the world by respondents, as well as the interpretation by researchers. This should be included in the analysis to a far greater extent as it is now. In addition, each research study is determined by (theoretical) assumptions made explicit in varying degrees, which are influenced by the contact with respondents as well. These processes should be made more explicit, but even then the concept of 'reality' remains questionable for supporters of these movements. **Institutional ethnography** is interested in the relationships between the macro-level of institutions and the way in which these affect the micro-level of respondents. Finally, **narrative research** investigates the way people use stories to represent them and give meaning to their life and surrounding world.

Scientific disciplines using qualitative research methods are, for example, cultural anthropology with the ethnographic method as main working procedure, sociology with the well-known grounded theory method, as well as biography research and discourse analysis, philosophy with the phenomenological method and finally, humanities with methods such as biography or narrative research, or discourse analysis. Additionally, case study research might be mentioned here as well, whose roots lie in social demography and social geography. In the meantime though, it has become an interdisciplinary method, particularly used in organizational and policy-oriented research (Braster, 2000).

In all of these approaches and methods the qualitative interview, as a means of collecting data, can play a role. The interpretation of the interview, the way it is conducted and the relationship between researcher and respondent will differentiate, depending on the approach or method that forms the starting point for the research project.

In the next section, the position of the qualitative interview within the most dominant methods is characterized.

In the **grounded theory** method (GT), based inter alia on the ideas of symbolic interactionism, the interview is often used. In a research project, conducted according to the principles of GT, the first interviews have an 'open' and 'exploring' nature. The researcher is interested in everything the respondent would like to share about the phenomenon under investigation. Once several interviews are held, data-analysis will commence as well as reflection on the first analytic results. The next interviews might even be less open in nature because the interviewer would like to explore certain themes which resulted from the first interviews. On the other hand, he might still aim to explore the phenomenon further and as such keep his interviews open and exploratory. In a following cycle of interviews the researcher might focus more in-depth on certain themes which resulted from the first cycle. The interviews will be more structured and might even be done in accordance with the tree-and-branches model, cf. Chapter 3. In a next cycle of interviews, the researcher might investigate whether themes that resulted from previous analyses also apply to different types of respondents. He might then again either choose for an explorative interview or a more structured one.

In the **ethnographic method**, stemming from cultural anthropology, the researcher often stays in the field for longer periods of time and participates in the daily life of respondents. This method is based on the idea that different cultures can only be understood in-depth, if one resides there for extended periods of time to collect all the information that is present, i.e. 'fieldwork'. Typical of this approach is the use of different data collection strategies such as observation, participation, interviewing, photographing or video filming and collection of other information. In doing so, a distinction can be made between 'formal' and 'informal' interviews. In formal interviews the researcher makes an appointment and questions are designed beforehand. If possible, the interview is recorded and the researcher will transcribe it as literally as possible. Informal interviews are interviews conducted during fieldwork or during participant observation. They are often not prepared but arise spontaneously during interaction between the researcher and the person(s) in the field. If possible, the researcher takes notes on these interviews in short keywords and transforms these into elaborated fieldnotes afterwards. Otherwise, he will make his fieldnotes purely from recollection. These informal interviews can either be of a very open character or the researcher might ask very specific questions regarding matters that are currently happening or happened earlier. As such, the investigator often does not have a recording or verbatim reproduction of the informal interviews conducted.

In **phenomenology** as a method, originating from a movement within philosophy, the emphasis is on the individual's environment and his experience. The aim is to understand the essence of an experience; in philosophy typically done through a thought experiment. In empirical research, the attempt is to find this experience through the use of interviews and the writing out of the experience (Maso in Evers, 2007). The aim is to highlight multiple layers of an experience, if possible starting from the pre-reflexive, that is to say, the part of the experience which is not conscious yet, and surface each layer into the whole conscious experience. Within phenomenology, different traditions appear, such as transcendental phenomenology, hermeneutical phenomenology and existential phenomenology (Holloway & Wheeler, 2002:170-178). Each of them has different accents in the research methodology[8]. For example, an existential-phenomenological research on solitude focuses on defining the essence of loneliness in relation to the responsibility of the self, while a transcendental-phenomenological approach is interested in tracing different meanings of the experience of solitude. A very open interview in a familiar environment with attention to the equality of the relationship with the respondent and much room for elaboration are essential in this approach.

In the **narrative method**[9] the open interview plays a crucial role. The emphasis is not so much on the experience of a feeling or phenomenon; instead the emphasis is on the display, on the configuration of a story, or on an event within a certain context. For instance, someone can start with the occasion that resulted in the event, followed by the elements that are of interest for the subject matter, how

---

8. The concept 'methodology' is used to indicate the primary logic and theoretical assumptions that guide a research endeavour. This concept is to be differentiated from the concept 'method', which indicates the working procedures used in a research endeavour, i.e. interviews, participant observation, document analysis, etc. Method then, is considered to be stemming from methodology (Bogdan & Knopp Biklen, 2007:35).
9. The biographical method is part of the narrative method.

matters evolved, and finally, outlines the present situation. Perception certainly plays a role as architect of the story but it is not the most important drive of the interview. The interview can be structured by using the respondent's' chronology as a focus, e.g. from toddler to infant, teen-ager, adult, or senior, or by taking a certain event during the respondent's life and investigate this in-depth.

In a **case study**, the qualitative interview is used in addition to other methods of data collection, comparable to ethnographic research. Here, one case is under scrutiny, both in-depth and widthwise. This could either be a department, an incident or a specific group. The researcher would like to learn as much as possible of this case in order to understand how matters work, how processes progress, how interaction takes place, and so on. For example, in policy research case studies are commonly deployed to evaluate the execution or implementation of a policy measure. In such a case study, key informants are often contacted for an interview: the initiator about the occasion, the implementer about the development and execution of the process, and a participant about whether or not an actual change has occurred. In addition to the case study that deals with one case, there are also multiple case studies compiled. In a multiple case study, several cases are either compared or contrasted to each other.

1.4   Methods of collecting data in qualitative research

As was previously stated, interviewing in this book is regarded within the context of qualitative research. An important feature of data collection in qualitative research is its open and flexible nature (Maso & Smaling, 2004). The researcher is attuned to what occurs in the field. In doing so, he might choose to start in a totally open manner. If so, he starts with a period in which he 'learns' and is exploring the environment. Only after this first phase will he explore matters more in-depth, or design his tproblem statement in more detail. On the other hand, he might structure his research project immediately after the start and describe in advance what information he would like to obtain and how he will approach the fieldwork. Such a strategy is often taken in commissioned research because of the tight schedule. In all modes of qualitative data collection, the emphasis is to do justice to the examined subjects as much as possible (Smaling, 1990). In doing so it is important to let the subject speak and not to distort the data, so valid and reliable results[10] can be

---

10. Internal validity, a widely used quality concept in qualitative research in brief implies that the interviewer and the respondent are talking about the same thing, and that the topic that is discussed is what the researcher would like to know according to his problem statement. On the other hand, internal reliability implies that members of the research team agree intersubjectively on the interpretation of concepts and results and that these are used in a consistent manner. For further details on procedures to increase internal "validity and reliability see Maso and Smaling (2004:68-73) and Seale (2000).

obtained. To achieve this, the researcher might 'keep book' in some kind of log, that is to say, a report in which all the choices made with regard to data collection and the investigation process are kept up-to-date. Subsequently, parts of this report might be included in the official publication, to ensure transparency on how decisions were taken, how data were interpreted, and how important concepts were obtained. At the end of this chapter we will elaborate on the validity and reliability of data.

There are various methods and techniques available in qualitative research to collect empirical[11] data. They are successively:
- Participant observation;
- Interviewing;
- Collection of documents, i.e. letters, diaries, notes, reports, newspaper articles, etc.;
- Collecting visual material, i.e. photos of objects, persons or situations, video-shots;
- Collecting of sound recordings, i.e. radio and television broadcasts, tape recordings of conversations or interactions.

In using the first two methods, the researcher directs to a great extent the nature of the data he collects. He influences both type and content of the data. In the other methods mentioned, the researcher does not always determine the content, as they may already exist. Thus, he selects texts, audio files, or images that others have put together in terms of content. In addition to existing photos, videos and tape recordings he can also capture such data himself. Of course, the method of selection is of crucial importance in such cases. We will not elaborate on this for now. The most important thing is that information is gathered about a specific part of social reality and that this information is the starting point for analysis and reconstruction of that social reality.
Below, these different methods of data collection are discussed briefly to delineate the position and context of qualitative interviews with regard to them.

Participant observation is often called the oldest form of qualitative research. Researchers use their own body, specifically their senses, and mind as the main resources to observe. They themselves are the research instruments. Participant observation means the researcher participates in the everyday life of his subjects and captures his observations in some form. Participation may take different forms and depends on the role the investigator chooses on location. In general,

---

11. We use the term 'empirical' to indicate systematic observations, whether or not done through the senses, in the empirical or social reality ('t Hart, Boeije & Hox, 2005), or a reproduction of them. In qualitative research it is habitual to gather information on a phenomenon in its natural surroundings.

four roles are distinguished: (a) complete participant, (b) observing as a participant, (c) participating as an observer, and (d) complete observer (Gold in McCall
& Simmons, 1969).

While participating to a larger or lesser extent in the life of the people examined,
the researcher needs to document his observations, including conversations, in
order not to forget what he heard and saw. This is done in so-called field notes
(Bogdan & Knopp Biklen, 2007; Emerson, Fretz & Shaw, 1995). It will prove difficult to write down all you have heard and observed and, therefore, parts of social reality will be disregarded. For this reason the advice is to complement fieldnotes with other methods of data collection, such as interviews and the collection
of existing information. Roughly, fieldnotes can be divided into two types:

• Jottings: (fast) notes to yourself; reminder notes made during or after short observation sessions of 15-30 minutes. The researcher records broadly what happened. These notes are created in such a way that they provide guidance to
  work them out more elaborately at a later time. An observation session can
  take more than half an hour but all that happened in that stretch of time cannot be remembered in detail. Therefore, it is advisable if it is not possible to
  write down keywords while observing, to withdraw from time to time from
  the scene, record some details in keywords and then continue with the observation.

• Descriptive fieldnotes: these are the real fieldnotes. This is the detailed report
  of the observation session, which was jotted down in keywords earlier. Someone relatively unfamiliar with the research setting is able to comprehend these
  notes. These fieldnotes are produced shortly after the event observed, preferably the same day, otherwise the following day, by using previously created
  jottings. This report is an extensive account of what happened, how it went
  about and what was communicated, sometimes with additional pictures,
  maps and drawings for better comprehension. It is best to use a chronological
  order in fieldnotes. Between [ ] or in a different textual colour, the researcher
  will add his thoughts, assumptions or prejudices about the event or persons
  participating and what struck him during the session. These additions are
  sometimes recorded in so-called reflective notes and as such form a third category of notes.

Interviews are the most commonly used method of data collection in qualitative
research. They can be done in several ways. Interviewing may also be less time
consuming than participant observation, depending on the type of interview
used. In comparison with participant observation, interviewing is somewhat
more structured and delineated. The researcher might determine the data slightly
more as compared to participant observation but this depends on the extent to
which he would like to steer the interview. The qualitative interview will not be
dealt with extensively here; in Chapters two to six and in part II of Evers (2007),
many aspects of it are discussed. Before an interview can be conducted though,

some necessary preparations should be made first. These are discussed in detail in section 1.5 and Chapters three to six.

Nowadays, a large part of communication is done through **(digitalized) documents**. The Internet can be consulted on almost any topic. Through the Internet a large number of text files, written on a wide variety of topics, is accessible. For example, the search engine Lexis Nexis enables researchers to collect newspaper articles on a particular topic in a defined period. The same applies to documents of a different nature. An important difference with participant observation and interviews is that other people write these documents and that the researcher has no influence on their content. As the information is almost infinite and each definition has an element of randomness in itself, it is important to clearly justify the selection criteria for the documents.

Depending on the research problem, documents can be collected as independent data or as supplementary material to observations or interviews. For example, complementary to an interview, the minutes of a meeting might be collected, or a nursing file on a patient. Sometimes they are really complementary to the information obtained in the interview, but on the other hand these data might confirm or contradict the interview data which contributes to the validity of the dataset. These documents are often not analyzed in the same detail as the interviews. They are used to supplement and to verify, so are a form of data triangulation.

A next strategy for data collection might be **sound or video recordings**. This can both apply to existing recordings or recordings the researcher creates or lets someone else create in the context of a research project. In most cases this will entail a combination of audio and video recordings, e.g. a video registration of a situation that is examined, an audio recording of interviews, educational films, television programs, or documentaries. These might all be analyzed separately or in relation to each other. In addition, it is possible to analyze sound recordings only. This may be a recording of interviews, telephone calls or other types of conversations: radio interviews on a delicate subject, recordings of meetings or conversations in a doctor's office. For example, we asked workers at eight mental care-settings in the Netherlands whether they wanted to record the intake interviews that they have in their own practice for us (De Boer, 1994). These data were collected in 'naturally occurring situations' (Silverman, 2006). For such data it is also necessary to develop a selection and analysis strategy beforehand, otherwise the researcher runs the risk of collecting data which are not suitable for the selected analytical methods.

1.5   DESIGNING QUALITATIVE RESEARCH

Visually, a qualitative research project might resemble the diagram below:

Diagram 1.1 The course of a qualitative research project

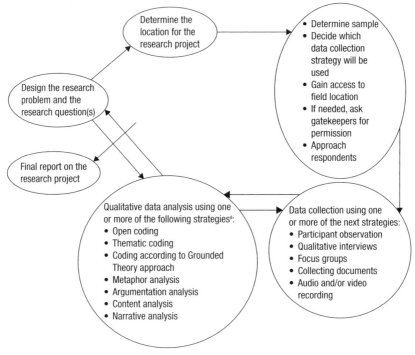

ᵃ For a description of some of these strategies see Evers and Van Staa (2011)

Next is a brief explanation of the various components of the design, preceding the data collection

Research question and goal

Any research project starts with a question, problem or topic that is interesting to the researcher. The first step then is a literature search, as he would not like to re-invent the wheel but wishes to build on knowledge already present on his sub-ject. Depending on the time available and whether the objective for the investiga-tion is practically-oriented, theoretically-oriented or both, the literature review will be more or less extensive. The literature review enables him to formulate his research question sharper and set the research objective.

The **research question(s)** formulate(s) the central query the project will deal with and as such provides the aim for the research. Typical for questions within qualitative research is that:
- An 'open' question line is guiding the research;
- It is often only possible to get to a more final wording of the research questions at the end of the investigation, as these questions are regularly adapted to interim results in the several cycles of data collection and analysis.

In this respect, qualitative research differs from quantitative research, in which the research question that was formulated beforehand is mostly final. In qualitative research this it is not possible, as the researcher would like to learn from the field while he is investigating. For example, the research might focus on a sub topic during the course of the investigation because it appears that this sub topic is more important than was foreseen. Or, the direction of the research might change slightly as findings indicate that unforeseen matters are quite important for the question in general. In such a case, the research question will be adjusted.

Qualitative research questions often appear as 'how' or 'what'-questions, they are 'holistically' oriented and search for information on processes, experiences, strategies, feelings, effects, behaviour, perceptions, motivations and so on.
Based on the main research question, some **sub-questions** might be formulated which are further elaborations of the main question. Similar to the main question in qualitative research, these sub-questions will be 'how' or 'what' questions but they might be more specific. For example: What strategies do people with multiple sclerosis apply in asking relatives for help?

The **research objective** differs from the research questions. In the research objective, the aim of the project is stated. This might be broader or might go further than the answer to the research question(s). A research project might aim for different goals. These may include:
- Obtaining knowledge or seeking information; the goal is knowledge acquisition;
- Contribute to theory or refine an existing theory; the goal is theory construction;
- Informing people; the goal then is spreading knowledge and educating people, for example about the consequences of a certain illness;
- Supporting people in making a choice; the goal is practice-oriented, for example to help people in making a choice for a certain treatment;
- Influencing a certain process (of change): the goal is action-oriented, for example during the refurbishment of an organization.

Once a research goal and matching research questions are formulated, the researcher might indicate which theoretical movement seems best to use in examining these questions. In choosing methods for data collection and analysis, it is best to be transparent about the paradigmatic or pragmatic position that guides the project.

Determine the location
Typical of qualitative research is that the researcher collects the data himself and thus will be present at the research location. It is important to think about where to find the desired respondents. Especially if participant observation is considered, this is an additional focal point during the design phase of the project. The choice of location is first and foremost determined by whether or not information which fits the research question can be obtained there, but secondly whether or not it is possible to get access to that location. This can sometimes be difficult and it is, therefore, recommended to think carefully about this in advance, especially if a location is considered with gatekeepers[12] present. The choice of location and its accessibility can to a certain degree determine the validity and reliability of the data. Often the gatekeeper determines whom the researcher can approach as respondent and this can affect the sample frame negatively. On the other hand, in choosing the location wrongly, people might be reluctant to participate and if the researcher has finally found someone willing to give an interview, this might be the wrong person or the question can no longer be appropriate for the available respondents. In both cases, the researcher reconsiders his sample frame, the research questions or both.

Once access is gained or granted to a certain location, this still does not imply that people within this site are prepared to participate in the research project. This again might require a great deal of effort from the investigator. The gatekeeper often claims that sufficient respondents are available but in practice they still might be reluctant to cooperate, or they prove to be wrongly selected by the gatekeeper. For example, there might be too much similarity between persons, or most people selected prove to assess the policy, which is under scrutiny, in a very positive way.

Sample frame in qualitative research
In qualitative research, the researcher will mostly look for participants in a targeted manner, the so-called **purposeful or purposive sampling**. Targeted sampling – as counterpart of at random sampling – means that respondents are selected deliberately and not randomly or through calculation of probability, as is

---

12. The concept 'gatekeeper' is used for persons that determine access to potential respondents. For example, this might be a secretary in an organization if you would like to interview the manager, members of a board of directors if you would like to interview employees, committee members if you would like to interview the members of their association, parents if you would like to interview children, or doctors if you would like to interview patients.

usual in quantitative research. Purposeful sampling can be done based on certain premeditated criteria, criterion based sampling, or on the basis of interim analysis of collected data, which leads the researcher to search for respondents who can either confirm, complement or overcome these interim results. The latter is named theoretical sampling.

In a criterion-based sample certain criteria are set to be met by respondents that are to be interviewed. For example, women who are diagnosed with depression by a psychologist, who are between 35-40 years old, work four days a week and have two children at primary school. Formulated this way, the researcher is looking for a very specific group of people. If a group of respondents is searched for, who must meet certain criteria like the ones stated above, that sample is known as a homogeneous way of selecting people. If, however, the researcher is interested in all aspects of depression in a broad sense, he should search across people in a more heterogeneous manner. For example, he might try to include an older man, a young girl and a middle-aged woman, etc. What these people have in common is their experience of depression. In this way, the research will probably result in a larger variety of knowledge concerning the concept depression. It is a less in-depth, and more breadthwise approach in comparison with the first method of sample selection.

1.6   THE ROLE AND IMPORTANCE OF REFLECTION IN QUALITATIVE RESEARCH

Qualitative research cannot be envisaged very well without reflection as an inextricable part of the entire research process. This surely is partly due to the fact that the researcher himself plays an important role in the entire investigation; he serves as a research tool in it. It is also related to the proximity to respondents and the continuous need to respond to what is occurring in the research process in which reflection is not only an aid, but also a necessity to keep track of the quality of the research. Below, a number of times when reflection on what is occurring is specifically important are mentioned.

First of all, at the start of the data collection and, more importantly, during and after the interview, **reflection** is important. Upon deciding to interview a certain group of respondents, it is important for the researcher to examine his **assumptions about this group**. It is essential to write these assumptions down and not just to remember them. Writing about them will make the researcher formulate them more precisely and this adds to his awareness of them. This thinking and writing about his assumptions might be repeated later on in the research process in order to describe any additions that surfaced later on surrounding the premises about the research group or topic. During data collection, the researcher would be wise to 'bracket' these assumptions, i.e. putting them aside consciously.

By doing so, he tries to prevent approaching the respondent based on his presumptions or prejudices. Placing one's assumptions in brackets should be done **before formulating the interview questions**, as these formulations may initially have been influenced by the assumptions of the researcher. In this reflection then, it is important for the researcher to note his implicit image of the people who will be interviewed.

Moreover, an openness to and reflection on comments of other people during the investigation process is habitual. These comments can both be received on a personal level and on a research level. During an intensive fieldwork period, the **balance between distance and involvement** might be seriously jeopardized. In (anthropological) technical literature the term used is 'going native', that is to say that the researcher identifies himself too much with the investigated group. The Dutch investigative journalist Stella Braam experienced this at first hand when she did undercover participant observation amongst addicted drifters in Amsterdam, The Netherlands. She became so involved in her fieldwork that she herself became addicted to drugs. At a conference in 2003 (Evers, 2004b) she reported that she should have organized guidance during her fieldwork period. She had needed someone to share her experiences with during fieldwork, such that they could have dissuaded her from over-commitment and might have drawn her attention to the use of drugs. This does not imply that the researcher will be restrained by such comment, but telling the story inevitably implies a step backwards, thinking and reflecting.

In addition, we believe that the balance between distance and involvement also is something that the researcher himself needs to give careful thought in his **reflective memos** and this not only applies to observation. It equally applies to , but the chance of intense involvement here is slightly less, as the contact is limited to one or a few face-to-face encounters. Intense involvement is much more an issue during participant observation and has to do with marking limits and at the same time being involved with respondents empathically.
In the quest for balance between distance and involvement, **ethics** play a role as well. Research is never unselfish, just as it is in the interest of the researcher to collect good information, the respondents have their own interests. They might try to use the researcher to work for them. In selecting respondents, in assessing the information they provide, and while reflecting on your performance in the research project, it is very useful to think about interests the various parties involved in the research might have, including your own (Evers, 2003).

1.7 CONCLUSION: THE RELATIONSHIP BETWEEN DESIGN AND DATA COLLECTION STRATEGY

As was shown in the preceding paragraphs, designing a qualitative research project does not happen overnight and there are many aspects to consider. In practice, the design is often neglected and we, therefore, propose to give it much attention. The progress of the research project and the extent to which it answers the research question(s) is closely connected with the preliminary work at the beginning. Both words 'Art' and 'Skill' from the title of this book are very appropriate here: the Art is only possible if sufficient Skill is present and applied!

2 | THE QUALITATIVE INTERVIEW: FEATURES, TYPES AND PREPARATION

2.1   WHAT IS QUALITATIVE INTERVIEWING?

The qualitative interview, also known as open, unstructured[1], semi-structured[2] or in-depth interview, is very similar to an ordinary conversation. However, it differs in some respects (Morgan, 2003, Rubin & Rubin, 2005):

1. The interview is a research tool, i.e. a deliberate process to collect information, which is then analyzed by the researcher, in the context of a research question, and of which the results are published.
2. The researcher determines the topic for the interview and intentionally selects the persons that are going to be interviewed, possibly through intermediaries.
3. Both strangers and acquaintances are interviewed.
4. The researcher leads the interview, addresses topics deliberately, and explores these in depth with the respondent(s).[3]
5. The answer is not known in advance, i.e. it is not presented to the interviewee by the interviewer.
6. The respondent determines to a large extent the size and type of information given.

To achieve this, one can pursue **five goals** in a qualitative interview:

Depth and detail
Depth and detail are somewhat overlapping categories, but they are still separate goals to strive for. In seeking more detail, the aim is to collect more information concerning every aspect of the topic under scrutiny. Mostly, probing is done within the topic. Depth is reached by searching for an answer, that transcends

---

1. A number of writers are opposed to the term unstructured. In their opinion, the deliberate nature of a research interview will always cause a certain amount of structuring (Benney & Hughes, 2003; Whyte, 2003).
2. A semi-structured interview is sometimes seen as a kind of qualitative interview although it is significantly less open than an in-depth, open or unstructured interview.
3. Depending on the type of interview, the researcher is more or less in control of the interview.

the superficial. Here, the interest lies in the particular meaning of a statement for the respondent.

If the respondent has told the interviewer that he had fun going out the day before, then the interviewer will look for detail through probe questions focusing on what exactly it is that made yesterday a nice evening. One can further explore what makes an evening out fun, by asking about other nights that were less or even more successful. Depth is achieved by determining the influence of a fun evening on the respondent, what it means in his life to have a fun night out.

Nuance

When looking for nuance, it is assumed that reality is not black and white. Something is often only partially true, or it is true in certain circumstances. Nuance implies different levels: someone can like something very much, or love someone unconditionally, but is that always true and under all circumstances? Nuance is obtained by probing. For instance: Are there times when you do not like something? How do you love someone unconditionally? Do you always do this to the same extent?

Liveliness

Liveliness is brought into the interview by formulating questions in such a way that they create room for the story the respondent might want to tell, or examples they might want to share. For instance: Can you describe such a situation for me? Can you give me an example of that? It means the focus is not only on looking for factual or rational answers, but the interviewer is also creating room for the emotional or perceptual aspects. For example: You have just told me about that situation at work, what happened there? How did that situation feel to you? What did it do to you?

Richness

If an interview is rich in information, it contains many different ideas and themes. The respondent has been given the space to elaborate on the various aspects of a subject. As such, the width of the subject is covered. To accomplish this, one might use probes, i.e. stick with what has just been said and elaborate on that, or ask follow-up questions, i.e. return to a new theme which was introduced by the respondent earlier, and ask him to elaborate on that. For example, in a research project about job satisfaction, a probe could be: You have just said that it is particularly important in your current job to be accurate, and that this was the reason you applied. Are any other aspects important to you in a job? A follow-up question could be: In the beginning of our conversation, you described yourself as a job-hopper. Could you elaborate on that?

Contrasting qualitative interviews with other forms of information gathering

Earlier, it was suggested that the qualitative interview is different from a normal conversation. It differs from other forms of information gathering and exchange as well. For instance the journalistic interview, talks with a counsellor, or contact with fellow-sufferers from some disease are all information-gathering conversations, but without the purpose and research methodology applied in a qualitative interview. The qualitative interview has practical or scientific pretence[4] and a robust methodological format, the other forms of information gathering do not.[5] The relationship between parties, mentioned in the examples above, are different from a research interview as well. In all these examples, the stakeholders benefited from the interview in one way or another, ranging from media exposure to mutual tips on the best treatments. In a qualitative interview, clearly the researcher benefits most (cf. Baakman in Evers, 2007). He is the one that would like to gain knowledge and because of this he looks for certain people whom he assumes are knowledgeable. At the same time though, respondents often also benefit from the interview. It can give them new insights or information, and even self-understanding.[6] Additionally, it can evoke deep emotions on the part of the respondent , due to the topic, which is being explored in-depth. To the interviewer, the interview can bring new insights as well. At the relational level, it can also create a bond between the researcher and the respondent, which can continue after the investigation (see Jonker in Evers, 2007).

2.2   DEFINING THE QUALITATIVE INTERVIEW

In the box below, some descriptions of the qualitative interview were collected. They are placed in alphabetical order by author(s). Some commonalities are found:
- Purposeful gathering of information: there is a research question;
- Differentiation of roles between interviewer and interviewee: the researcher asks questions and the respondent answers;
- Openness of possible answers: answers are only checked on their relevance to the research question content, not on their content, and

---

4. We distinguish practical and scientific research because of their aim. Scientific research is geared towards theory building, while practical research is geared towards solving some practical problems. Both, however, use scientific research methods and we think both should be done in a scientifically sound way, although their emphasis will differ.
5. Except for maybe the classical investigative journalism, which comes closest to the qualitative interview, but even then the pretence is breaking news, i.e. signalling a problem and not solving a problem through knowledge creation, as is the goal in applied research, or theorizing, which is the goal in scientific research.
6. Especially in action research, which aims to change an existing situation together with the respondents, this might happen. In mainstream qualitative research, which will not have change as its primary goal, still the interview might result in having some effect on the respondent.

- The depth with which information about the experiences of the respondent is collected. This is opposed to quantitative research, which mainly works with closed questions and answering categories.

Differences between authors exist as well. These are reflected in the nuances of defining the qualitative interview. For instance, Ellis et al. write from a more postmodern, feminist interpretation, Grbich also focuses on power differences, Gorden writes from a more quantifying, i.e. controlling viewpoint. Additionally, Rubin and Rubin especially focus on the communication process and less on the techniques to be applied.

Different definitions of a qualitative interview
Different definitions of the qualitative interview are possible. A selection:

'(…) we introduce interactive interviewing as an interpretive practice for getting an in-depth and intimate understanding of people's experiences with emotionally charged and sensitive topics (…) we view interviewing as a collaborative communication pro-cess occurring between researchers and respondent, although we do not focus on valid-ity and bias. For us, interactive interviewing involves the sharing of personal and social *experiences of both* respondent and researcher, who tell (and sometimes write) their stor-ies in the context of a developing relationship. In this process, the distinction between 'researcher' and 'subject' gets blurred. The feelings, insight, and stories that researchers bring to the interactive encounter are as important as those of the respondent.' (Ellis et al., 1997:121, indented in original)

'Interviewing is conversation between two people in which one person tries to direct the conversation to obtain information for some specific purpose.' (Gorden, 1998:2)

'The aim of conducting interviews is to gain information on the perspectives, under-standings and meanings constructed by people regarding the events and experiences of their lives.[…] Interviewing styles vary from something approaching an informal conversation between friends (where issues of equality have been carefully considered) to a formal interrogation. (…) The notion of a friendly conversation implies an estab-lished relationship with some form of reciprocity. Although this may well be achievable in some situations, in others it is an overglorification of the power-laden, awkward in-terchanges that actually occur. The process of gaining information through interviews contains an underlying assumption that interviewer and interviewee actually under-stand one another: that the signs and symbols used are meaningful to both, and that both share the visual images evoked and the interpretations applied. (…) Another as-sumption underpinning the interview process is that a response to a question will bear some relation to the 'truth' of the person's understanding and knowledge of the issue. It is vitally important that due consideration be given to the disturbances caused by the researcher focussing on one aspect of a person's life experience (...)The issue of power in the interview process must also be addressed. Postmodern interview techniques allow the researcher to take a decentred position, although this has not been accepted as readily in research as it has been in literature (...)The issue of power in the interview process must also be addressed.' (Grbich, 1999:85-88)

'An 'interview' is seen as a form of conversation, 'where a person – the interviewer – will limit himself to ask questions about behavior, [feelings], beliefs, attitudes and experiences (...) to one or more others – respondents – who are mainly confining themselves on answering those questions.' (Maso & Smaling, 2004:50)

'Responsive interviewing (...) emphasizes that the interviewer and interviewee are both human beings, not recording machines, and that they form a relationship during the interview that generates ethical obligations for the interviewer. In the responsive interviewing model the goal of the research is to generate depth of understanding, rather than breadth. The third characteristic of responsive interviewing is that the design of the research remains flexible throughout the project.' (Rubin & Rubin, 2005:30)

In this book, **qualitative interviewing is defined** as:

A qualitative interview is a form of information gathering, in which the interviewer queries one or more respondents, based on a research question. Thereby, the interviewer creates space for the respondents to dwell – in their own words – on the perceived facts, their experiences, the meaning they give to the subject of investigation, nuances regarding it and its possible effect on their lives. In doing so, the interviewer tries to understand and thoroughly investigate the respondents' world.

The qualitative interview reflects a **certain epistemological viewpoint** as well, which is expressed in the definition used in this book, and some of the others, presented in the box above (see also Booth & Booth, 2003; Evers, 2003, and the contributions in Evers 2007, Part II):

- Inviting respondents to talk about their experiences in their own words creates comprehension of, and knowledge about people.
- Interviewing implies a relationship between researcher and respondent, which creates mutuality.
- Within the relationship between interviewer and respondent, power and gender issues might play a role.
- On an epistemological level, there is an ethical position linked to the qualitative interview. Besides, quality standards regarding the research efforts, the humanity of the relationship between researcher and respondent, and the completeness and accuracy of data and research, are issues to be taken into account.

Good qualitative interviewing assumes certain knowledge and a considerable amount of practice; it involves both Skill and Art. In the following sections, we will discuss general features one should take into account when considering a qualitative interview. In subsequent chapters, this is taken further for both individual interviews and focus groups. We assume that, once the researcher has decided what his research problem is, he will first determine who the target audience is for the project. Only then can he decide what type of interview is preferable.[7] For that reason, we have classified the following sections accordingly. We will begin with the type of respondents he would like to interview.

2.3   RESPONDENTS COME IN SHAPES AND SIZES

It may seem obvious but the differences between people play a role in preparing a qualitative interview. In interviewing older people, the researcher's aim might be to frame his interview differently from when interviewing younger children or psychiatric patients. He might approach political or financial elites differently from marginal groups. We do not mean to say that one group deserves more respect and appreciation than the other, on the contrary! The point is that he responds to the reality of that particular respondent, such that the trust or *rapport* he is able to build between both of them is likely to develop. Ultimately, he would like to achieve a high quality interview and entering into the world of the respondent during preparation will help him achieve this. In Chapters 3 to 6 we will have a closer look at the aspects to be taken into account when approaching and interviewing certain types of respondents.

2.4   WHO ARE YOU, AS AN INTERVIEWER?

As mentioned before, it is important to ask who the future interviewees are and how best to respond to their world. Likewise, it is important to ask who you are as an interviewer. During a qualitative interview, the interviewer will often have to improvise and follow the story of the respondent. The subject of the research project and the type of respondent that is going to be interviewed, will require him to take the role of an empathetic interviewer or a more confrontational type of interviewer. The personality of the interviewer also has to be taken into account. A confrontational interview style does not fit everyone; at the same time some people are not comfortable with a very open and following interview style either. For example, people familiar with interviews by the media will require a more confrontational style than people who do not have such experience. On the

---

7. This sequence is somewhat artificial because sometimes other motives determine which type of interview will be used, such as the time or budget available for the project.

other hand, studies of people with terminal cancer are more likely to require a more empathetic tone, as opposed to a confrontational interview style.

Reflecting on one's interview style is an integral part of the qualitative research process. The Skill Learning Cycle by Gorden (1998:3), which visualizes how theoretically the process of refining interview skills will progress, can be of help in doing so. Below is an adapted version, in which some of the main points are changed.

Scheme 2.1 The Skill Learning Cycle (Adapted version)

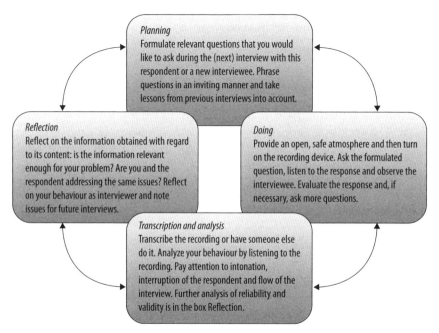

Planning
Formulate relevant questions that you would like to ask during the (next) interview with this respondent or a new interviewee. Phrase questions in an inviting manner and take lessons from previous interviews into account.

Reflection
Reflect on the information obtained with regard to its content: is the information relevant enough for your problem? Are you and the respondent addressing the same issues? Reflect on your behaviour as interviewer and note issues for future interviews.

Doing
Provide an open, safe atmosphere and then turn on the recording device. Ask the formulated question, listen to the response and observe the interviewee. Evaluate the response and, if necessary, ask more questions.

Transcription and analysis
Transcribe the recording or have someone else do it. Analyze your behaviour by listening to the recording. Pay attention to intonation, interruption of the respondent and flow of the interview. Further analysis of reliability and validity is in the box Reflection.

In the following sections, ways to structure the interview using its content, type and several kinds of questions are discussed. Besides these techniques, the person(ality) of the interviewer can also assist in structuring it. In addition to ways of structuring the interview, Chapters 3 and 5 mention different roles that can be utilized.

2.5   EXPLORATION, INTERVIEW TYPES AND QUESTIONS

Qualitative research is often associated with **exploration**. Along that line of thought, it is assumed that qualitative researchers need little time to design their research, as this occurs during the research project. In our opinion, it is exactly the improvised nature of qualitative research, which would benefit from a thorough preparation. This improvising quality of qualitative research concerns the understanding of the world from the viewpoint of the respondent. It requires great flexibility on the part of the researcher and should not be confused with **exploratory research**, which is something quite different. In exploratory research, the research question itself is quite open, as there is not a great deal of knowledge available on the research topic yet. In that case, it is indeed not possible to design all the details of the project beforehand. The difference between both of them can be found in their relationship towards the research design. They share flexibility and openness towards new insights and viewpoints.

In the next section, types of interviews, types of interview questions, and the similarities between different forms of qualitative interviews will be discussed.

2.5.1   *Interview types*

Qualitative interviews can be characterized along several dimensions. The number of respondents who participate in it can be used as a starting point for the type of interview to conduct. The content one would like to cover during the interview can also be used as the basis for the design. Closely connected to this is the degree of structure that is planned for the interview. Both issues will be discussed briefly in this section. In Chapters 3 and 5, which deal with the design of the individual interview or focus group, they will be discussed in more detail.

Individual versus group interviews
In qualitative research there are different types of interviews. The most striking one perhaps is that between an individual interview and a group interview. In individual interviews, their name is already quite informative: typically one person will be interviewed at a time, sometimes two.[8] The individual interview is discussed in more detail in Chapter 3. In contrast, group interviews[9] are generally conducted with six to ten persons simultaneously. These are called focus groups, if the investigator selects the target respondents using certain shared characteristics, such as profession, gender, or income. In general, participants do not know each other in a group interview, although sometimes the researcher deliberately selects people that are familiar with one another (Kitzinger, 2003). In

---

8. Although the researcher aims to interview one person, sometimes family members or other persons are present at the moment they have agreed to an interview. Such a situation is always difficult: will he continue the interview as planned, or move it to another time? This will depend on several factors; for a comparative case study see Boeije 2005a.

9. Nominal and Delphi group techniques are not considered to be group interviews in this book. In the first, the group is separately questioned and the results are circulated throughout the group. In the second, the input in the group is not seen during the process, as participants sit at different computers, and only see the input of each member anonymously on screen while consensus is sought. (Finch & Lewis, 2004:173, De Ruyter and Scholl, 2001:54).

Chapters 5 and 6 group interviews are extensively explained. The question when to choose one or the other, remains. The following table provides more insight into that matter.

Table 2.1　Choosing between an individual or group interview (Lewis, 2004; Morgan, 1998a)

	Individual interview	Group interview
The aim of the data is to:	• Hear in-depth personal stories • Discover the personal context and understand it • Explore some themes, both in-depth and within that depth in all their detail	• Explore a particular topic broadly; data are partly defined through the group process, refined by it, and possibly reflected upon • Discover the social context of matters; how people think and talk about a particular topic • Explore the diversity of opinions • Learn how interaction within a group influences the opinion of people • Think towards a solution creatively in a group session. The latter is mostly done in applied research.
Research subject	• Complex processes and issues such as motivation, decision making, effects and results • Exploration of personal issues or themes that reflect social norms • Very sensitive topics	• Abstract, technical and/or conceptual topics can be dealt with by using special techniques or giving additional information • Complex processes and issues such as motivation, decision making, effects and results • If understanding or exploring differences between people is the goal • Topics that benefit from expressing social norms • In certain sensitive areas only possible if the group is carefully composed and has an experienced moderator • Empowerment or action-oriented objective
Research population	• Respondents who cannot travel or are unwilling to do so • A geographically very dispersed group • A highly diverse group of subjects • When power issues are a concern • If communication is difficult for the target group	• Respondents who are willing and able to travel and would like to join a group • A group which is geographically centred • Respondents who share a background that relates to the subject • Respondents who are not inhibited by the group process

Cultural versus thematic interviews

Based on the research question and objective, the type of interview deployed is either focused on so-called cultural issues or on thematic issues (Rubin & Rubin, 2005). In cultural interviews, the concern is with everyday life, with what people do and what they transfer from generation to generation. Usually, these topics are not very explicit. It is quite difficult, therefore, to formulate and pose questions regarding these matters. Interviewees are mostly not very aware of them and find it hard to articulate them. It is often useful to combine these interviews with (participant) observation as a means of data collection. In thematic interviews, the concern is a subject that is often defined and is placed in a certain time frame, e.g. a particular event.

Interviews by their structure: trees, rivers and sluices
The next distinction made is based on the structuring of the interview. This can be done through the interview model, which emphasizes a certain style of questioning. Rubin and Rubin (2005) suggest three models for structuring the interview, which are followed here and will be further developed in Chapter 3. They use the metaphor of the locks of a sluice which are going to be opened, a meandering river and a tree with branches. Each model has its own interview style, which has consequences for the type of questions used. In Chapter 3, these models will be discussed in greater detail.

Crane and Angrosino (1992:18) distinguish the non-directive interview and the directive interview and attach these to the phases of (ethnographic) research. Usually, if the researcher is new to the field or still in the exploratory phase of a project, they will start in a non-directive way, asking general questions. This can be compared to the opening-the-locks model of Rubin and Rubin. Once the researcher has become more knowledgeable on the topic, he might like to interview in a more focused way, selecting specific themes beforehand. This can be compared to the tree-and-branches model. Another distinction is that between formal interviews versus informal interviews,[10] particularly in a field setting (p. 19, and Van Gemert in Evers 2007[11]).

2.5.2   Question types

As was discussed earlier, the researcher has a certain aim with his project and designs a matching research question. Research questions, however, are not the

---

10. This distinction between a formal and an informal interview within ethnographic research is fundamentally different from the models discussed here, or from what is usually meant by an open interview. An informal interview during ethnographic fieldwork is a conversation that occurs spontaneously during the (participant) observation sessions of the field worker and for which no detailed questions were prepared. It is usually not recorded, but written down later as extensively, and maybe even as literally, as possible. In these informal interviews the investigator also questions matters observed just now, or matters that were discussed or observed earlier, but without preparing them beforehand. There is no meeting place arranged for this informal interview, it takes place spontaneously and it is up to the researcher to make optimal use of the time (Wolcott, 2005).

11. The contributions in Part II of the Dutch version of this book are examples of interviews in which the research question or the target population determines the style and model of the interview.

same as interview questions. This mix-up is often seen in research designs. Research questions are usually charged with a certain level of abstraction and may contain (theoretical) concepts which are not used in everyday conversation. Formulating interview questions can be seen as a form of operationalizing[12] the research question. Starting from the research question, some major themes or concepts can be identified. Often, these themes can also be subdivided. Those (sub) themes or concepts are to be reworded into interview questions.

In **designing** the **interview questions**, the following points can be considered:
- On a communicative level: interviewing means having a conversation, the researcher would like to interact with the respondent in order to receive information;
- On a relationship level: they would like to develop a relationship with the respondent which is as open and equal as possible in order to receive authentic and valid information;
- On a perceptive level: appropriate language for the respondent should be used, ensuring that they understand the questions posed. Besides that, they should feel they are regarded a worthy interlocutor;
- The situation the respondent is in: sometimes it is difficult for a respondent to speak freely, for example, because of an authoritarian corporate culture, because they live in a dictatorship, or come from such a place.

Interview questions ought to be formulated in such a way that the interviewee can answer them quite easily. That is to say, they need to understand clearly what it is the researcher would like to know. The way interview questions are formulated may have a serious impact on the information obtained.[13]

Questions for different purposes
In formulating interview questions, a distinction can be made between questions regarding their form or regarding their content.

In its form, the question may be open or closed. Furthermore, the extent to which the question is directive, adds to its form. A question can also be formulated in a

---

12. Operationalization is the rewording of an abstract concept such that it can be investigated empirically or observed in its natural surrounding.
13. This is known as social desirability of answers (Babbie, 2004:250), in which the respondent anticipates in his reply to what he thinks the researcher expects. In such cases not only the wording of the question is important, but also the self-awareness and assertiveness of the respondent and the degree of *rapport* that the researcher can achieve during the interview.

broad or narrow sense. Furthermore, it can refer to the respondent's own experience in a direct way or in a more indirect manner[14].

Regarding its content, an interview question can be a main question, a follow-up question or a probe:

- **Main questions** start and guide the interview in the direction, chosen by the researcher beforehand.
- **Probes** are used in response to answers given by the interviewee. They are used for clarification or to get a deeper understanding of the subject. They remain with the topic at hand.
- **Follow-up questions** explore the implications of answers from the interviewee to main questions or probes and are designed on the spot. They adopt new themes, which were first introduced by the respondent in one of his answers.

Other issues which need attention in formulating the interview question are its range, the amount of directivity used, and the level of abstraction involved. The following chapters will elaborate on how to work with these types of questions.

2.6   THE USE OF ELICITATION TECHNIQUES AND CONVERSATION GUIDES

In the sections above, question types, interview models, personal qualities of the interviewer, and the type of content one is looking for with the interview have been addressed. The importance of the designing phase of the research project was emphasised as well. In our opinion, sufficient time should be spent on designing the project in order to achieve high-quality research data. In practice, this entails reflection on possible questions *and* answers, and careful design of the questions which will be used. In order to achieve this, conversation guides can be developed to help monitor the main subjects during the interview. Depending on the type of structuring desirable, this can for instance be checklists, topic lists, protocols or interview guides.

In the methodological literature a variety of terms is being used for conversation guides. A number of them have been collected in alphabetical order in the box below. What is striking, is that they do not seem to vary much in their content. Besides that, sometimes even the same terms are used for matters that are quite different, as is reflected in the box below. One starts to wonder whether it consti-

---

14. Questions that might be threatening or that address a taboo, can sometimes better be formulated indirectly, e.g. through a hypothetical example. The intention then is to let the respondent answer them anyhow and in doing so involve his or her experience. If not so, the researcher can try to use follow-up questions or probes to address the experience or knowledge of the respondent, in order to avoid a validity problem.

tutes a contribution to methodological knowledge in general to constantly introduce new terms.

A forest of terms for conversation guides

Checklist: to Rubin and Rubin (2005:149), this is simply a list of themes or topics the researcher would like to discuss in the interview. These lists are constantly changing as
the project progresses because new issues surface during the interviews which seem
more important than the issues one started with. If different respondents are selected
for sub-topics, it might be useful to make a comprehensive checklist of all the themes
that should be dealt with, and assign these to different people.

Guide: a transcending term for a conversation guide, which may take various forms:
more or less developed and for a more exploratory or a structured interview (see Patton, 1990:283 ff; Heldens & Reysoo, 2005:121). During the project, the form of the
guide used can change (Rubin & Rubin, 2005; Schensul et al, 1999). Knopp Biklen and
Bogdan (2007) reserve the term 'guide' for an observation guide; they use the term 'interview schedule' for conversation guides.

Interview Guide: includes a description of the issues that will be raised during the interview and sometimes even a timetable for each topic or specific elicitation technique.
This last point is specific for market research. The questions themselves can be formulated in more or less detail (De Ruyter & Scholl, 2001:29; Wester & Peters, 2004:60).

Interview protocol: in this format, the key questions for the interview are written down
verbatim. Such a protocol can even be presented beforehand to the respondent or gatekeepers (Rubin & Rubin 2005:147). In Dutch language, the term 'protocol' is sometimes
used for a written interview record or a transcript (Baarda, De Goede & Van der Meer-
Middelburg, 1996:72; Wester & Peters, 2004:89).

Interview schedule: a list of questions to which the researcher would like specific answers. Usually, such a guide can only be formulated if one is familiar with the culture
of the respondents. It is a good way to obtain missing information and to tie up loose
ends (Crane & Angrosino 1992:58; Wolcott 2005:108) or as a format for a semi-structured interview (Schensul et al, 1999:153).

Jottings: notes, taken in keywords during an observation session or an interview, on
which the researcher would like to elaborate in subsequent probes or follow-up questions (Rubin & Rubin 2005:148).

Topic list: a translation of the 'central concepts of the researcher regarding topics that fit
the framework of the respondent'. This is done in the form of a main topic, with an introduction and a few issues on which to probe further (Wester and Peters, 2004:61 ff).

> Wester and Peters see the topic list as a conversation guide for a quite well structured form of interviewing. The topics are introduced to respondents in a uniform manner. The topic list is tried and refined beforehand through pilot interviews.

Besides the conversation guide, which reproduces topics and possible questions designed beforehand, the researcher might also consider to use specific elicitation techniques[15], e.g. pictures, photos, inversion, etc., during the interview. Chapter 3 mentions some examples of elicitation techniques for individual interviews. Chapter 5 does the same for focus groups.

2.7   SIMILARITIES BETWEEN QUALITATIVE INTERVIEWS

The different types of respondents, structuring mechanisms, interview questions and tools which have been distinguished so far, require a slightly different approach each time. In Chapters 3 to 6, this will be illustrated on the level of design and in practice. However, the different types of qualitative interviews also have some similarities, which will be dealt with later.

A qualitative interview is preferably a situation reminiscent of a 'normal' conversation. The **difference** lies **in listening and questioning**: a researcher listens much more intensely and detect important themes, words, intonations, silences and non-verbal behaviour to include these in his line of questioning.

> 'In qualitative interviews you listen as to *hear the meaning* of what is being said. You develop skills to listen carefully, sentence by sentence and word by word. Qualitative interviewing requires listening carefully enough to hear the meanings, interpretations, and understandings that give shape to the worlds of the interviewees. (…) The depth, detail, and richness we seek in interviews is what Clifford Geertz (1973) has called *thick description*.' (Rubin & Rubin, 1995:7, italics in original)

To achieve this, the researcher focuses on fewer topics in the interview than in a normal conversation, allowing space for sufficient probing into themes in order to gain an in-depth understanding.

Qualitative interviews especially focus on discovering experiences and perceptions of respondents, and their interpretations and organisation of the world that

---

15. Elicitation techniques are specific ways of interrogating or the use of specific aids. They are used to motivate respondents to provide information. They differ from normal methods of questioning because an additional stimulus is applied within the question or a tool such as a photograph, picture or assignment is used to get specific information.

surrounds them. Therefore, it is crucial for the interviewer to be attentive to concepts, symbols or metaphors that are important to the respondent. These can aid in understanding their interpretation of the world. As classifying respondents or events according to academic theories is not so much a goal, qualitative interviewing requires openness, interest, respect for the opinion and perception of the respondent, listening intensely and a systematic attempt to *understand* the respondent[16] (Maso & Smaling, 1998; Stroeken 2000[17]). **Openness** to new meanings and viewpoints is part of empirical phenomenology, also known as 'bracketing', or placing your own experience, as a person, interviewer or researcher, between brackets (Beekman & Mulderij, 1983). For a critical discussion of this concept see Maso, 2002). Culture[18] can be a useful strategy to map the world of the respondent. This can be done by (a) questioning new members about what they learned when they first became members of the group, (b) asking about the meaning of words and phrases, (c) awareness of symbolism and metaphors and inquiring about these, and (d) putting one's own culture into perspective.

The content, rhythm, and thematic choices in the interview need to be adapted to the individual respondent. Therefore, the qualitative interview is quite **unpredictable and dynamic** and requires great flexibility of the researcher.
The respondent is a full conversational partner[19], not a passive information provider. The interviewer must actively respond to the respondent: what is his knowledge of the subject, is he a tight-lipped person or very talkative, does he speak much about himself or not? In this sense, the qualitative interview differs considerably from the standard survey approach, in which basically every respondent, regardless of his or her attributes, is asked the same question.

---

16. 'Understanding' (translated from the German 'Verstehen', a term introduced by Max Weber, see Bogdan & Taylor 1975:2) refers to more than the literal hearing of words. The focal point is trying to understand what moves a person and trying to understand the world from their point of view by empathising.
17. Although Stroeken writes from a psychoanalytic frame of reference, this book is quite instructive for qualitative researchers. Evers (2002) discussed it in KWALON 20, vol. 7, No. 2, pp. 50-52.
18. Rubin and Rubin (2005) agree with Van Maanen and Barley (1985) by using a rather narrow definition of culture: a set of solutions that a group of people has developed to deal with certain situations and solve the problems attached to them (underlining by JE). This definition of culture offers them the opportunity to apply the concept of culture broadly, not just for ethnic groups, but for organizations, families, or states as well. In short, for any group of people who share something. In our opinion, the definition Kloos (1981:14) uses offers a broader framework, as input for an interview: 'culture... the whole of habits, institutions, symbols, ideas and values of a group'.
19. Some researchers prefer the term 'conversational partner' because this emphasises the active and equal role of the respondent and creates the awareness in the researcher that he is seeking for the experience of the respondent. See Laslett & Rapoport (2003) for a description of how to address equality while monitoring the validity at the same time, and striving for balance on the empathic level.

The personality of the researcher, his or her baggage, and prejudices play an important role during the qualitative interview. Therefore, according to Rubin and Rubin (2005), **neutrality** is unattainable for the researcher. It seems though as if they use the concept of neutrality to stand for objectivity, which indeed is not possible in social sciences. To us, seeking to balance involvement and detachment as a researcher and at the same time acknowledging the different views, i.e. understanding them without taking a stand, is what we would call neutrality. Therefore, to us neutrality is certainly not impossible, but definitely difficult to attain. Although in our experience **empathy** guides the interview, it does not imply such involvement that the researcher cannot see the negative side of the respondent or does not dare to report this. Since it can be difficult to empathise with certain types of respondents, the qualitative interview might teach the researcher something about himself as well: unexpected anti-feelings or sympathies he might have, or prejudices he carries.

As the researcher initially is the greatest investigative tool, reflection is an important part of qualitative research. **Reflection** on the own performance is an essential part of the qualitative interview. How does the researcher respond to answers given by the interviewee?, How does he formulate his questions and how much room is there for the respondent's story and digressions? The bias,[20] irritability, anger, fear, enthusiasm, concentration and fatigue of the researcher greatly affect the interview. Laslett and Rapoport (2003) indicate that they structurally monitor the transference and countertransference during the project. We would advise you to be aware of this, as well as of your own cultural assumptions and language and ensure that you do not impose your opinions – implicitly or explicitly – on the respondent. Strips (2000) formulates some helpful suggestions on handling this. During the interview it might help to probe in-depth on the context, which surrounds the respondent. This then can help in gaining insight into the way the respondent interprets events and how they apply meaning to them.

---

20. *Bias* is the prejudice of the researcher, which distorts his perception. Bias may include preconceptions about others, which everyone has, but it can also be facilitated by a particular view of science or the literature used for the project, which may be reasoning in a certain direction. It is important to get to know your own bias as much as possible. A convenient aid in getting there is letting someone you trust query you on certain topics: ideas you have about the research and its topic. What do you expect to find?, Reasons and motives you have for doing this research. What is it exactly that you would like to investigate? and What are you aiming for? Van Keken (2006) mentions Socratic dialogue as a technique for doing this.

Another crucial aspect for a good interview is the amount of ***rapport***[21] the inter-viewer can obtain with the respondent (Maso & Smaling, 1998:105-107). In Chap-ters 3 to 6 (and in Part II of Evers 2007) the subject will be discussed extensively. For data quality in both the first and second stage[22] of the research project, the level of ***rapport*** that the researcher can achieve is highly important. Therefore, it is obviously crucial to pay enough attention to establishing a trustful relationship with the respondent by showing calmness and openness.

The most important data are not always taped on the **recording device**. The con-versation which occurs before starting the recording device, or what is said when the device is stopped, is sometimes much more relevant to the research problem than what was said during the recording. Please ensure this information is noted down as comprehensively as possible and at the first occasion, to avoid your memory letting you down. Related is the deliberate mention of matters '**off the record**' by respondents. This might place the researcher in a dilemma; what sta-tus do these data have within the whole project? This type of information often highly increases his understanding of the subject, but can he also report it? Each case has to be weighed in its own right. It might be useful to discuss with the re-spondent whether the information can be presented in a somewhat disguised form, if it were a pity not to include it. It is certainly worth scrutinizing the rest of the data again, in search for similar statements. If this statement occurs when the data collection is still ongoing, the researcher could cautiously check it against other respondents.

2.8 REFLECTION ON THE QUALITY OF THE INTERVIEW

It is advisable for the researcher to **systematically reflect** on the quality of his in-terview each time he completes one. This not only tests the data quality, but it al-lows him to increase his interview skills as well. In Appendix I a questionnaire is available for guidance in this process of reflection.
In this section the factors that affect the quality of the information will be dis-cussed. In short, this entails a) communication: the method of questioning and answering, and the mutual perception therein, and b) the resulting relationship between the researcher and the respondent.

---

21. *Rapport* is the trusting relationship that develops between the interviewer and the respondent. Ini-tially it is the task of the interviewer to ensure conditions for this are present, but it is obviously a matter of reciprocity whether it will succeed. It is generally accepted that there has to be sufficient *rapport* for a good exchange of information, in which the respondent feels safe enough to share more sensitive issues with the interviewer.
22. Laslett and Rapoport (2003) argue that the degree of *rapport* also has an effect on the depth of in-formation in second instance; the respondent remembers details after the first interview that they did not immediately recall, e.g. as a result of the relationship with the researcher.

Communication

Aspects that increase the quality of communication during the interview are: the kind of questions asked and their formulation, the perception people have of each other and the answers given. The question asked affects the information the researcher receives. As an interviewer he would like to obtain information from the respondent, but the **type of question**[23] or the **nature of the question**[24] may cause the respondent to use an evasive response strategy. This undermines the validity of his data; Silverman (2006) calls this an error of the third kind. Due to the question researchers ask, a false picture of reality is given. An evasive answering strategy can occur because of the way the question was formulated but it can also occur with questions on sensitive topics such as sex, alcohol, fraud, etc., or in certain target groups such as adolescents, people with little education or people at the margins of society.

Regarding answers given, Gorden (2003) mentions two aspects that can affect the quality of information. Firstly, the **memory** of the respondent is to be considered. A respondent can give an incorrect answer to a simple question because he does not know the right answer at that moment. This then is not done to give a better impression or a different one from the actual situation. The incorrect answer is sometimes corrected later in the interview because the topic occurs again or because he suddenly realizes that an incorrect answer was given earlier on. This can be seen as part of the 'stream of consciousness': the longer a subject is discussed, more layers of consciousness are opened and the respondent remembers more about it. This creates a situation of 'retrospection'[25] whereby the memory is activated through the interview, and one stimulus activates a chain of memories about how they reacted on that particular stimulus at the time of confrontation with it in the past.

The second aspect that can affect the quality of information is – sometimes fast – **generalization**. This can be used as an evasive strategy. Gorden discovered this when he interviewed people about their role in a disaster. In his research, people dodged the question by providing answers in general terms because they were ashamed of their behaviour during the disaster. When given general statements by respondents, alarm bells should ring: how valid is this statement? The interviewer can try to investigate this by enquiring about details. In generalizing statements, errors often occur which the interviewer can try to find and correct by probing and asking follow-up questions. He might use empirical reference: did the respondent experience this himself? Is this the personal opinion of the re-

---

23. The *type of question* refers to its technical formulation: is it formulated in a suggestive, directive or closed way?
24. The *nature of the question* refers to the topic: what is the question about?
25. The term was coined by Merton (1990:23) for his focused interview technique.

spondent? Does the respondent speak from his own perception or experience? Generalizations are especially used as an evasive strategy if people are reluctant to discuss certain issues too deeply. They might think the subject too sensitive, or there is insufficient *rapport* for this question at that particular moment. Generalizations are also used to disguise a lack of knowledge or experience, i.e. the wrong respondent, or if they do not understand the question, i.e. wrong wording of the question by the interviewer.

Besides the method of questioning, memory issues and generalizations, the **perception** people have of each other is also important for the kind of answers that the interviewer receives. Firstly, the image the respondent has of him affects the nature of the information he shares. It might be that the respondent is withholding information because he expects disapproval. If the researcher creates a situation in which the respondent feels that it is safe to put forward the less heroic side of things, or even better, that they can highlight both negative and positive aspects, this will result in a more realistic picture of their world. Second, the observed or perceived socio-cultural distance between researcher and respondent can affect the quality of the information. It may also play a role in withholding information. These are perceptions in terms of differing wealth, differences in educational level, cultural differences, language differences, and dress codes. The latter especially affects young people or occurs in circles where great importance is attached to external appearance. Information can also be withheld in relation to privacy, see for example Booth and Booth (2003).

The relationship with the respondent
During the interview, two – sometimes more – people come together who may not know each other. Whether a good exchange of information will occur, depends in part on the role that the interviewer takes during the interplay between detachment and empathy and the *rapport,* which is a result of that. Depending on the type of research, the interviewer on an empathetic level, has a choice between four roles according to Maso & Smaling (1998:104). They derived these roles analogue to the way the researcher functions during participant observation:
- The detached interviewer or full observer. He asks questions, shows little emotion, does not strive for (deeper) contact with the respondent;
- The partially detached interviewer or participant observer. He poses questions, probes answers, shows emotions and compassion, but keeps a certain distance;
- The empathic interviewer or the observing participant. He poses questions, builds rapport and seeks an equal relationship in the interview;
- The fully empathic interviewer or complete participant. He poses questions, feels for the respondent, there is an equal relationship and the interview resembles a very personal conversation.

This classification of course should be understood as a continuum. During an interview the interviewer can switch between these four roles. The first and fourth positions seem to be less adequate for a good interview, but they sometimes occur in research. Generally, an interviewer alternates between the second and third role. It is advisable to consider the role that you would like to pursue as an interviewer in advance. Reflecting afterwards helps to see what you did in real terms.

The second aspect that was mentioned, *rapport*, is about the trust that arises between the researcher and the respondent. The researcher might strive for an atmosphere of confidence during the interview as soon as possible. This enhances the probability that the respondent will share important information, and that this information corresponds to reality. This again stimulates the validity of his research.

From under-rapport to over-rapport

Maso and Smaling (1998:105 ff) express their doubts on the notion of *rapport*; according to them the researcher usually defines the term in a one-sided and strategic way. The researcher must win the confidence of the respondent in order to obtain the necessary information, and the risk of 'over rapport' receives more attention than the reciprocity of the relationship. To refine this, they propose a nine-graded scale:
- Under Rapport: the respondent has little or no confidence. This will harm the methodological quality of the research.
- Benevolence: for each mutual contact, minimal benevolence is required. In a research situation this causes a lack of quality in the communication between researcher and respondent.
- Trust: it is necessary that the respondent will trust the researcher enough to grant him an interview.
- Mutual trust: in certain types of research, e.g. participatory or action research, it is required that the researcher has minimal confidence in the project and in those who operate it, in order for it to be successful.
- Dialogue: there is more reciprocity in the contact and symmetry in the relationship, if compared to the previous grades of rapport.
- Collegiality: in this version, a certain dual loyalty exists within the contact, which is not necessarily present in a dialogic relationship.
- Friendship: in friendship, the mutual loyalty is even greater, as well as the liking of each other, which also plays an important role.
- Love: Love is blind, but it can make you see more. According to Maso and Smaling it does not necessarily causes over-rapport.
- Over-rapport: over-identification with the respondents. 'Going native' is a term from cultural anthropology and a form of over-rapport. The researcher then is trying very hard to be part of the group he investigates; he denies his own background and identity. The result is that he is not listening, watching and analysing in a critically enough manner.

For a research project not all these gradations – although informative – are relevant. In general, the researcher would like to strive to be somewhere in between collegiality and trust. According to Maso and Smaling both friendship and love can lead to over-rapport. In our opinion, in a research setting in which many interests are involved, collegiality might also lead to over-rapport. Sometimes a respondent also becomes a friend, as was illustrated by Jonker (in Evers 2007). In other cases the researcher is not be able to create symmetry in the relationship, even though he tries. Especially social and/or cultural distance may hinder this, as well as the time available for the research project. We do not think this is always problematic. The researcher cannot just eliminate social or cultural distance within a few hours or a few conversations. The point is that he is still bound to do whatever is possible to let the respondent feel sufficiently at ease, such that there is enough room for the exchange of confidential information.

2.9   FINDING AND APPROACHING RESPONDENTS

In finding and accessing respondents, it is assumed that the researcher already identified the target-group based on his research question. In this section, the practical issues that are important in approaching people for the actual interview will be discussed.

Qualitative interviews are often done face to face, that is to say the respondent is interviewed in person. Interviews can also take place by telephone or on the Internet[26]. We limit ourselves to the **face-to-face interview** in this book. This kind of interview to us has a number of important advantages, not in the least the proximity to respondents and the possibility of observing their body language. Therefore, it provides other information than a telephone or Internet interview, though not necessarily better.

The fact that the interview is a living encounter has several consequences for finding and accessing respondents. First, they must be willing and be able to meet the interviewer in person. Some issues may prevent that. People may find it annoying to talk about certain subjects face to face, or to do so in groups. This might be induced by shame, wanting to keep their anonymity, not wanting their acquaintances to know that they participate, inability to travel due to physical or financial constraints, or inability to have long conversations.

---

26. Interviewing via the Internet can be done by e-mail or in online chat rooms. Knowledge of software and hardware is required, as well as a customized interview strategy. For a detailed discussion of advantages and disadvantages and the need to adjust the approach to technical, legal and ethical terms see Mann and Stewart (2002) and Murray and Sixsmith (2003).

Approaches via institutions
However, how does one find those people for the research project in the first place? A basic search criterion is whether the intended audience is institutionally embedded, e.g. within an association, organization, club, church or mosque, ethnic group, union, school, etc.. The potential respondents can then be found along that path. Telephone books and Internet can offer addresses of those institutions. However, usually in such cases the researcher has to deal with gatekeepers: people who monitor the access to the actual target group. In organizations this might be managers or directors, but family members can monitor access to the respondents as well, for example, parents of the children the researcher would like to interview. The moment the researcher has to deal with **gatekeepers**, he needs to realize that the gatekeepers are the ones that introduce him to the respondent. They might get a more or less distorted message to the respondent which the interviewer must check and redress during his first meeting with the respondent. In addition, there are power issues between gatekeepers and respondents that can determine the progress of the research. Gatekeepers can also select and refer persons who turn out to be the wrong kind of respondents or they can be selected in a biased way. Therefore, the researcher needs to ensure he gives a very precise description of the kind of respondents he is looking for to the gatekeepers and try to find a gatekeeper that is not in a hierarchical relationship with the respondents he needs.

Approaching respondents by other means
If the respondents are not institutionally embedded or if the researcher does not wish to find them through these means, several other channels are available. For instance, chat rooms on the Internet, places in public spaces where the target group can be found, e.g. on the street, in shops, coffee shops, or disco, and advertisements in newspapers or free local papers. These are all ways to find people for the research project.
The researcher can appeal to people on the street. He should ensure his introductory presentation is prepared, keep it short and to the point, and practice in advance in order to make this a successful strategy. If he approaches potential respondents through advertisements, he should ensure he has his introductory paper with him, so he can draw from it during an eventual telephone conversation. If he searches for people through chat-rooms, he might invite them in his introduction to contact him outside of the chat room. For instance, persons wanting to participate could contact him via telephone or via a specially created email address. In addition, a common technique in qualitative research is the snowball method: if the researcher has found someone, he asks that person if they know others who would like to participate, and these people can ask others again, and so on. The disadvantage of this method is that one often stays within a certain circle of people. The researcher can still look for new respondents during the interview phase, not only through the snowball method, but also by the other

channels mentioned because they can adjust the target based on interim analysis of the interview data.[27] Sometimes, it might be better to contact the respondents by way of a letter or e-mail before calling them or ringing their doorbell. Especially if respondents are expected to be suspicious of the research motives, an official letter with the logo of the organization from which the study is undertaken can be reassuring.

What should be in the introduction?
It has already been mentioned that the introduction should be short and to the point. Especially when the research is introduced orally, people must be able to understand what the research involves. Keep sentences short and in plain language, appropriate to the audience. They have to be told enough about the purpose of the research so that they know what they are participating in, but not so much that it can influence their answers in certain directions. Sometimes, the researcher even has to disguise some of the research purposes in order to prevent this, e.g. in evaluation research. Additionally, he should try to make his introduction enthusiastic. One way to do so is by letting people know how important it is to him that they are willing to participate. It can be useful to mention the importance of the research for them as well. The researcher does not have to share everything during the introduction; we experienced people deciding not to participate when we told them we would like to record the interview. We then decided not to mention this during the introduction anymore but to ask if we could record the interview just before it actually started. Of course, if they would then object to a recording, we would refrain from that.

Once respondents are willing to be interviewed, it can still fail. People get sick, they have forgotten, something came up, they drop out on second thought. It is important, therefore, to allow for unforeseen setbacks in the research schedule. For example, the researcher might want to look for more respondents than he needs during preparation, so he might have backup candidates available if people withdraw.

2.10   PLANNING THE PROJECT

Planning is a standard feature of a research project. Especially the data gathering period is planned too tightly on a regular basis. The research budget sometimes forces researchers to do so but the underestimation of the time needed for fieldwork is a considerable factor as well. Much tends to go wrong during the fieldwork period, so it might take longer than was planned, or additional respondents need to be recruited. In such cases, additional funding is often needed, which of

---

27. In the framework analysis, a method currently being developed by Evers, it is even a prerequisite.

course is not easy to obtain. So the researcher had better allow for setbacks when planning the project; they should add at least one-third of the time they calculated.

In planning a qualitative research project, especially the starting phase and the fieldwork phase with possible interim analysis followed by recruitment of new respondents, deserve attention.
Qualitative research often takes place on location, i.e. in the field. This can be in an institution or organization but respondents may need to be recruited in other ways, for example through an advertisement, as was mentioned earlier. This might already be the first stumbling block for planning because it can be difficult to estimate in advance how long it will take to get permission from the institution or organization or how many people will respond to an advertisement for an interview. It is best to try to get an indication of the time needed when writing the research proposal, so planning can be adjusted accordingly. The researcher might consider seeking permission from the institution or organization already during the designing phase of the project. It is more difficult to obtain this permission from respondents during the designing phase if the researcher needs to recruit them through advertisements. If they still cannot get consent, an estimate has to be made of the time needed to do so. Regular meeting moments of institutions need to be taken into account during the planning phase, as they may delay the planning schedule considerably. In health research, often a research proposal needs to be evaluated by an ethics committee first. This takes quite some time as well because there are many forms to be completed, after which the process of evaluation by the committee also takes several weeks. Depending on the type of research, ethics committees nowadays might ask for a contribution in the costs of evaluating the research proposal. The researcher should include this in the budget proposal.

2.11   Balance between problem statement, design and technique

In this chapter the qualitative interview was introduced in all its aspects. The characteristics, the type of interviews, which questions to use when, the link between the target group and the form the researcher chooses, and ultimately, how to approach the respondents were described. Clearly, the problem statement, the target group and the interview format chosen must be balanced. This means that the data collection technique is appropriate for the research questions, that the conversation guide covers them all and is tailored to the target group and that there is enough space and time scheduled for unexpected issues along the way. It is not entirely inconceivable that the researcher notices during data collection that matters are different from earlier expectations, or that a particular approach does not work with specific respondents. In such cases, he should be flexible enough to adapt the design, e.g. short conversations during observational sessions if it appears that long interviews are not appropriate for a particular group. This is the Art that complements the Skill. The following chapters will focus on the skill of designing the interview. Chapter 3 will discuss designing individual interviews; designing focus groups will be discussed in Chapter 5. The translation from Skill to Art is subsequently discussed in Chapter 4 for the individual interview and in Chapter 6 on focus groups. Chapter 7 will discuss the processing of interview data and the technical tools available.

3 | DESIGNING INDIVIDUAL INTERVIEWS

Before doing a qualitative interview[1], the researcher first needs to decide on which respondents to include, how much control he would like over the interview, what sort of interviewer he is himself, what aids he might need and whether he needs (extra) training or not. A number of these decisions of course will depend on the research question and goal, as well as on the time and financial resources available for the research project. We deal with all these decisions in the following paragraphs and will start with the impact of the research question on the choices he makes.

3.1 WHAT WOULD YOU LIKE TO FIND OUT?

For a qualitative interview terms like 'open interview', 'depth interview', 'unstructured interview ' or 'half-structured interview' are customary. Most authors see structuring of the interview as a function of the questions which are designed beforehand; the number of themes the researcher would like to address in the interview is a function of the need to structure the interview. As such, the structure of the interview might be interpreted as a two sided coin: on the one hand it resembles the way questioning styles are dealt with, and on the other hand it is determined by the type of information that is sought. We will elaborate on this below.
Other important factors are: the researchers's personality and the roles he takes during the interview or the style he uses. This will be dealt with in paragraph 3.8.

Before going into all these ways of shaping the interview, the question of what information he is looking for and what target group he needs to interview – his sample – to obtain it needs to be answered. This largely determines how the interview can run its course, as can be seen in the following paragraphs.

---

1. In this book the focus is on the interview as primary data collection method. As has already been said in Chapter 1, there are other methods of data collection and the interview is not by default the best choice. The best data collection method has to be decided for each research project, based on the problem statement.

3.1.1   What kind of information should the interview yield?

As discussed briefly in Chapter 2, during the interview the researcher might use
main questions, probes, and follow-up questions. To apply these various types of
interview questions well during the interview, he needs to have his research goal
and research question clear from the start. In designing a research project it is
helpful to identify all the concepts that are considered important in advance.
Drawing a conceptual model which relates the main concepts to each other and
defines the assumed relationships between them is a good way of determining
what seems essential for the research goal and research question.
In our experience, reading and thinking about a project suggests a growing number of important angles to pursue in an interview. The researcher has to choose
between these and in doing so, he might use what Gorden (1998: 12) calls the
'**usability test**' to decide which angles to pursue in the interview. In this test, he
asks himself: how will I use the information obtained from an interview question
and how useful to my project are possible or different answers to the question? If
he cannot answer this with regard to the topics he would like to address in his
questions, then those questions are of doubtful relevance for his research project.
Once he has decided which interview questions are relevant to his research objective, he can decide on the type of interview to pursue. He is then able to choose
between one opening question that covers all potential themes, or design several
key questions as an aid to conversation.

In the box below we give a notional example of ways to think about relevant
themes for an interview. Of course, you then need to think about the target
group for your project, in order to determine what interview model to apply,
what elicitation techniques you might want to deploy, whether or not to design
a conversation guide, and so on. All these techniques are dealt with in the following paragraphs.

Suppose Dutch Rail NS decides to use qualitative research to identify what motivates
commuters to use public transport. Hundreds of themes are conceivable in designing
possible questions for the interviews. To name a few: environmental considerations, fa-
cilities for working while travelling on trains, travel expenses, travelling allowance, opportunities to meet others, stress levels, and so on. Before such choices are made it is
important to establish an agreed project objective. Do NS plan to analyze the results as
an aid in designing advertising campaigns? Are NS aiming to promote greater use of
public transport? Are NS aiming to improve the quality of their service? This list of
possible research goals is by no means conclusive. Different interview questions will
be needed for each of these aims.

Imagine NS wanting to improve their services. Do they already have any preconceived ideas about this, and have they already excluded any specific items of service? Or do they have a very open mind, wishing to know everything passengers might conceivably wish during their train journey? In practical research of this kind the researcher often treads a very fine line between a solid research design and such factors as time constraints calling for a more structured type of interview, readiness to consider unexpected results, or a tight deadline.

If NS exclude all kinds of aspects beforehand, there is nothing to be gained in probing such issues. The researcher can, however, decide to tell his sponsor about the added value of qualitative research, which is precisely the identification of people's deeply felt perceptions and experiences and not so much their superficial opinions. It is thus highly important to define the research goal fairly precisely, as that is what determines the angles he will pursue in his interviews and the way he would like to structure them. In commissioned research, the interview sometimes needs to be more structured than wished for ideally. Whether or not this is the case, the researcher will always have to think about themes that might materialise and how he can address them in an open way. Our motto is: having an open mind about unexpected results does not absolve you from the duty to design you research well. It is precisely by giving very careful thought to the goal of your research in advance that you will find it possible to deal flexibly with unexpected situations during the interview.

3.2   WHO ARE YOUR TARGET RESPONDENTS?

Certain groups of respondents require adjustment of basic interview techniques. That is why we advocate asking yourself beforehand whom you are targeting. Try to gain more in-depth knowledge about them; this enables you to use that information in designing your interview. Certain **cultural perceptions** people may have can result in them applying different social codes to those the researcher is familiar with. He should take note of these ahead of time. This can apply to ethnic groups as well as professional groups, groups from differing social backgrounds, religious groups and so on.

Interviewing **mentally disabled persons** for instance, requires special preparation, adapted language and specific elicitation techniques (Kröber and Zomerplaag in Evers, 2007). These interviews should not be too lengthy. (Booth & Booth, 2003). The same applies in the case of **children** and **young people**. They do not have a very long concentration span, so keep it brief and go along with what is happening. **Elderly** people, on the other hand, often require more time (De Lange in Evers, 2007), as do **psychiatric patients**. Interviewing **elites** is a different matter; accessibility, planning and thorough preparation is of the utmost importance in such cases. (Baakman in Evers, 2007). They have little time available and expect the investigator to make good use of that time, having done his

homework in advance. Much information on elites is public, which means the researcher can find out much beforehand. (Zuckerman, 2003; Ostrander, 2003).
Power considerations play a specific role in interviewing elites and this sometimes makes it more difficult to control what is happening in the interview. This
specifically might be an issue in interviewing respondents who are accustomed to
a controlling position. Interviewing people from a **different ethnic group** might
result in specific demands on preparation, e.g. the need for an interpreter, the
dress code, not looking people straight in the eye, or specific attention to introducing the research question. Some people from ethnic groups[2] are difficult to find
or approach; the researcher needs to allow extra time in his project for recruitment. Other groups that are difficult to recruit are: politicians and other public
figures, sportsmen and women, celebrities and companies (Adler & Adler, 2002).
People of lesser fortune also tend to keep away from research, either because
they have something to hide, e.g. criminals, or because they have much to lose,
e.g. benefit claimants or illegal immigrants (cf. Van Liempt in Evers, 2007). People may be reluctant to participate because they have something to hide or belong to a secret society or because they fear repercussions or retaliation, e.g. abor-
tion clinicians or whistle-blowers in a company. People may also be reluctant because the research topic is sensitive e.g. finances, sexuality, drugs and alcohol, relational problems, or disease. In **recruiting difficult groups**, both access to the
group and overcoming possible resistance play a role. On both accounts it is essential that the researcher is perceived as trustworthy. In contrast to the unwilling respondent there is the all-too-willing respondent who can be found in new
elites or among long-forgotten veteran servicemen, frustrated individuals, naive
attention seekers, or those who have lost power but still have expertise.

Conclusion
What matters is that the researcher gets acquainted with the group of people he
would like to interview in advance in such a way that he is aware of certain
group features, e.g. accessibility, traceability, goodwill, social codes, the need for
a specific interview design or specific elicitation techniques. He can take these
into consideration in designing his interview and approaching the sample of people he would like as respondents. In addition to the technical aspects of the interview, i.e. the design, presentation is also of importance. In particular his use of
language must be suited to the research group. Physical appearance is something
to consider as well. He should try to adapt himself in terms of his clothing to the
people he is about to interview, without being overdressed, undermining his self-
esteem, or diverging too much from his own age group (Baakman in Evers,
2007). Researchers should not wear jeans or a dress if they never do so, but for
example, female interviewers should wear long sleeves and cover their legs if
they interview respondents with an Islamic background. The researcher should

---

2. In The Netherlands, this has been reported for Chinese, Moroccans, Turks and Hindus.

refrain from dressing as a teenager if he is middle-aged himself, but he might dress more casually than he normally would. The point is to adapt yourself in such a way that the respondent will not be offended or place you in a certain 'group' so that they anticipate their responses or refrain from cooperating in the research project altogether.

In the following paragraph determining the scope of the interview is dealt with and in subsequent paragraphs interview models and question types are discussed.

3.3   CULTURAL VERSUS THEMATIC INTERVIEWS

As already mentioned above, the research project starts with a problem statement that defines the research goal, the research question and the way the researcher would like to approach this. In Chapter 2 we stated briefly that he could choose either a cultural or a thematic interview, depending on the breadth and scope of the research question. If he is interested in the socialization and interaction patterns among youths, he applies a cultural interview. If he would like to know what precisely happened during soccer riots in Rotterdam, a topical interview is more appropriate. Hereafter we will deal more extensively with what this entails for the design, as it will reflect directly on the way he structures the interview.

A **cultural interview** explores the everyday, the cultural norms and habits. These are mostly not made very explicit but are transferred in the form of (unwritten) codes of conduct, proverbs and habitual behaviour through socialization, education, myths and stories. This type of interview is often difficult for that very reason. People find it hard to describe their everyday (habitual) reality and assume it is too dull for words. Your first task, therefore, is to let your respondent know that it is precisely this everyday life that interests you as a researcher. In cultural interviews then, few questions are formulated in advance. Rather, the investigator seeks to persuade people to relate how an event took place, or tell him a story with examples from their own lives. He can then probe on issues he would like to go into more deeply. In this type of research, fieldwork, i.e. (participant) observation is certainly advisable to inform and structure the interview. If doing research about youth culture, tag along with those youngsters or observe them unobtrusively in the public arena. The combination of observation and interviewing undoubtedly gives added value to data in this type of research and adds substance that can be probed in the interviews. If observation is impossible, a *tour question* can be formulated (Rubin & Rubin, 2005: 160), in which the respondent is asked for a step-by-step description of the event or process the researcher is interested in. From the description he can select examples or narratives to probe on in the interview.

A **thematic interview** is an interview that focuses more specifically on a defined subject and a given time period, such as a political event or a specific decision-making process. It is a kind of case study on the level of an interview: the researcher would like to know everything there is to know about a specific event, the what, how, why and when. In a cultural interview he is looking for the breadth and depth of the normal course of business and it gradually becomes clear which are the most interesting aspects. In a thematic interview, the 'problem' or the derogation of this specific case – at least in broad lines – is known in advance. Thus he can conduct the interview with a much sharper focus in comparison with a cultural interview, which is in essence exploratory. For a thematic interview, investing extra time in gathering information in advance from other sources is certainly advisable. Perhaps he is exclusively interested in this one case but he can understand and distinguish the case better if it can be compared with the 'normal' state of affairs.

If you have determined where you interest lies, you can choose the interview model that best fits your needs. We will deal with interview models in paragraph 3.5. However, first you need to understand the kind of questions that can be used during any interview.

3.4   SEVERAL KINDS OF INTERVIEW QUESTIONS

As mentioned earlier in Chapter 2, the researcher can make use of different types of questions during his interview. In the following paragraphs this will be explained in greater detail.

3.4.1   Question types according to their format

An **open question** does not contain any answering categories nor does it indicate the answering direction, the latter being directive or suggestive: 'Can you tell me how you came to choose this profession? A **closed question** implies the answer or only leaves room for a yes/no reply: 'Did you opt for this profession because of the contents or because of the salary?' The researcher strives for an open question as much as possible, but will not always succeed in doing this, as sometimes a yes or no question is inevitable: 'Were employment opportunities a reason for choosing this trade?' In doing so, he can then probe further on the answer he is given.

The **scope of the question**, i.e. wide or narrow, is a continuum of four dimensions. Gorden (1998: 33) distinguishes the actor(s) involved, the action, relevant relationships and the context, i.e. the location or the event. In each of these dimensions he can design the scope of the question as wide or narrow. An example of each degree of scope with regard to the actors involved: 'Can you tell me who were present when the fire started? Were you the only one present when the fire started?'

3.4.2   *Question types according to their content*

Main questions arise from the problem statement and are designed for each interview in order to structure it (Rubin & Rubin, 2005: 134-144). Main questions guide the interview along and they are often processed in a conversation guide. They must be sufficiently openly formulated to give the respondent an opportunity to show what is important to him/her, but focused enough to stay within the limits of the problem statement for the research project as a whole. Main questions 'translate' the problem statement into interview questions[3]. According to Maso (2006: 12), main questions have a different function; he refers to 'starting questions'. According to him, starting questions should be worded slightly more widely than the problem statement of the research project. His argument for this approach is that it is less confrontational and will generate even more information because of its broader wording. Maso's starting questions are clearly linked to the sub questions formulated as part of the research question. In the event that no sub questions have been formulated, only one starting question will be designed. Legard, Keegan and Ward (2004: 148) refer to 'content mapping questions': questions whose main purpose is to explore the research topic in a broad sense and to obtain relevant domains or themes within it.

Conclusively, each of the aforementioned question types differ somewhat. In general, however, they all have roughly the same intention: to launch the interview and ensure that it is moving within the framework of the problem statement. In future the term *main questions* will be used.

Probing is a technique, applied to bring *flow*[4] into the interview and at the same time resulting in more depth on a theme. The researcher asks for details or examples without changing the topic of conversation. By encouraging the respondent to tell him more about the subject, he signals that he is really interested in their story, thus helping to build the *rapport* needed to get a qualitatively good interview. Probing answers from the respondent for clarification or complementation shows that the researcher is a careful listener. The difference with follow-up questions lies in the scope of the question: with probes the interviewer stays within the stated topic and he invites the respondent to elaborate further or provide him with examples for clarification.

---

3. Before interviewing you will need to transpose the research questions into a format that responds to the social world and the language used by the respondent (= operationalization), thus enabling them to answer the interview questions.

4. We define *flow in the interview* (derived from Rubin & Rubin, 2005) as follows: the interview is following a smooth track in which there is room for silences, while the stream of thoughts that is triggered by the interview in both interviewer and interviewee is balanced. The interviewer adapts his behavior and stream of thought to that of the interviewee and keeps his own line of thought, to which he would like to refer to at a later point, separated by jotting it down in key words.

Follow up questions take matters a step further. These questions are designed during the interview, building on new or interesting issues that have been raised by the respondent. From these issues, the interviewer selects some that are interesting to him and designs a follow-up question that elaborates on what has been said earlier and explores the issue further. They provide the depth for which qualitative research is renowned. It is mainly here, in the follow-up questioning line, that discoveries are made! You need to listen quite carefully and remain very concentrated to hear, select and choose the right issues to follow up on. Probes often enable a deeper understanding of the issue. Follow-up questions extend and supplement the theme which could spawn entirely new insights. These can then be probed in turn, which will deepen your understanding of them.

Conclusion

In conclusion, when formulating interview questions, the following aspects need consideration:

Table 3.1   Points to consider in formulating interview questions

Formulating the question	Content validation of the question
Is the question open enough?	Do the interview questions completely cover the research question?
Is the question geared toward factual information (only)?	Are the interview questions set out in a logical sequence?
Are there any qualifying remarks[a] included in the interview question? E.g. good/bad, very, funny/boring, awful, slow, unbridled.	Do the interview questions reflect that information is sought on a certain topic and is there (enough room) for several aspects involved in the topic?
Do interview questions contain so called 'source effects'[b], meaning that they refer to something specific, i.e. a person, a specific statement.	
Are there any answering categories[c] in the question?	
Are there several questions enclosed in one interview question, i.e. serial or parallel ?	
Is the language in sync with the respondent group?	
Is the question clear and unambiguous?	
Is the question formulated according the theoretical framework?	

[a] Qualifications used in a question may lead to the respondent emulating them, either because he believes the researcher would like to hear this, i.e. social desirability, or because he cannot think of better wording which is more suited to his own experiences or feelings about the issue at hand. Qualifications are always a form of control that may sometimes be very suggestive. The interviewer will try to avoid them in his questions.

[b] Source effects have the same effect as qualifications: they steer the respondent in a certain direction. Sometimes that is exactly what the interviewer would like to achieve because it is about a specific person for example. So he will be alert in formulating his questions to avoid any source effects in them and will ask himself whether this is what he is looking for and whether it can harm the quality of his data if he is steering the interview in this way.

[c] Answering categories are possible answers that are already contained in the question. As such, it is not an open question being formulated but rather a closed one.

3.5   STRUCTURING THE INTERVIEW THROUGH THE INTERVIEW STYLE.
            THREE MODELS

In this paragraph we will elaborate on the three models already briefly referred to in Chapter 2. We start with the Opening-the-locks model.

Opening-the-locks
In the opening-the-locks model the researcher would like to obtain the widest possible insight into the subject of study, so that matters that require further exploration can be identified at a later stage of the research project. He designs just one main question or a maximum of two, to start the interview. These questions are formulated in such a way that they: (a) broadly define the area in which the interview will move, (b) do not refer to more specific issues within that area in which he is also interested, and (c) dig into the knowledge and experience of the respondent and explicitly refer to that and (d) are formulated in language that is clear to the respondent (Maso & Smaling, 2004: 88-89). In this interview model particularly probes and – to a lesser extent – follow-up questions are dominant. The main question, e.g. about decision-making processes in public administration, should be applied only to get the interview started[5]. This interview model is often used in the beginning of a research project, when the researcher is not yet so knowledgeable on the subject, or if he does not want to steer the direction in which the interview is moving at all, but just would like to set the boundaries of the overall topic. This model is the most exploratory of the three: he either uses it in the exploratory phase or if he is pursuing a narrative or a broad life history. The main characteristic of this model is that he is following the respondents' movements all along, no main questions – except the starting one – or follow up questions are used, only probing questions.

River
In the , the metaphor of several separate strands coming together in a flowing river to form one large flow is useful. The large flow may subsequently divide again into separate strands which come back together at a later stage. This metaphor might be pictured in an interview in which the researcher formulates a main question and in doing so stumbles upon a strand within the main flow of the river. He then follows this through using probes and in monitoring the answers he may discover several other interesting strands to dig into later on. If the flow of the current seems to have been dealt with exhaustively, an earlier

---

5. This does not mean that the main question is therefore less important, quite the opposite. It is rather difficult to design a good main question which on the one hand is specific enough for the respondent to understand what you are interested in, and on the other is sufficiently comprehensive to avoid sending him in a certain direction from the outset. Pay attention to the design of such a question and test it on friends or colleagues before using it in your interview.

strand is opened up again by designing a follow-up question on the spot. In this model, there is a sequence of probes and follow-up questions that increasingly elaborates on the previous questions. Together, they explore a specific theme in detail, excluding other themes that are potentially relevant. There is a risk that the interviewer ends in a narrow side-stream of the river that is less relevant than it seemed beforehand. This interview style is dominated first and foremost by the in-depth exploration but addressing subjects raised by the respondent earlier, at a later stage and exploring these in- depth supplement this in terms of width.

In the example mentioned earlier on decision-making processes in public administration, one could focus the question on disputes between departments. Not all aspects of the decision-making would be explored as they would in the tree-and-branches model, but only the description of disputes between departments and other players. Depth is clearly dominant in this interview model. In a life history that is aimed at a given topic in life, cf. a topical life story interview[6], such a style would also apply.

It will be clear that the opening-the-locks model and the river model both aim specifically at depth in the interview. However, opinions vary on what should be understood by 'depth'. In the box below we have selected different views of the matter. After that we will explain the most structured of the three models, the tree-and-branches model.

Depth in qualitative interviews

Qualitative interviews often are in-depth interviews but opinion varies on what depth means. We took a small selection from existing literature.

Johnson (2002: 105 et seq.) describes 'deep information' as:

- the search for knowledge and understanding on the level of group members or participants in the phenomenon examined. The research can obtain this information either as an outsider or as (ex-) member of the group;
- he defines 'deep' as understanding the phenomenon before common-sense-awareness; you would like to explore the limits of the phenomenon, which is implicit and hidden, and reflect on it.
- deeper understanding of a phenomenon tells you something about yourself as well, how your own background and (cultural) baggage determines your outlook;
- finally, depth also unravels multiple perspectives on the phenomenon; pay full attention to its complexity.

Gorden (2003:171) defines depth as: 'The 'depth' of any item of information depends upon its meaning for the respondent which, in turn, depends upon how he perceives the relationship between the information and the total social context in which it is given.'

---

6. Personal information E. Jonker.

According to Booth and Booth (2003: 23), a good in-depth interview leaves the respondent with the feeling that he was in control of the situation.

Merton and Kendall (2003: 253) were looking for maximum self-disclosure of the respondent on experiencing some stimuli offered. To Merton, the task of the researcher then is to monitor profundity. We see this as having both positive and negative sides to it. The researcher ensures the interview surpasses the superficial opinions but he does not dig so deep that the respondent is hurt as a result. If this might happen unexpectedly, then he offers assistance, at minimum in offering the opportunity to talk about it (cf. Maso & Smaling, 2004).

In short, the degree of in an interview is not a foregone conclusion and needs to be achieved by the researcher in each interview. Rapport and openness from the investigator play an important role of course, as well as the skill to probe.

Tree-and-branches
In the tree-and-branches model the research interest is seen as the trunk of a tree and the branches are the topics he would like to ensure are included in the interview. These are translated into main questions and are each designed with approximately the same degree of depth and, therefore, have more or less the same weight during the interview. The researcher might pay more attention to one branch than to others but all branches are addressed. Main questions as well as probes are dominant in this interview model. The aim is to find out how the individual parts, for example the different departments, the counties, or the civil organizations, impact on the whole, in our example project about decision-making in public administration. The width dominates the depth as interview aim in this model. For this interview model typically a conversation guide is drafted, cf. paragraph 2.5.3. This interview style is particularly suitable for practice-oriented research, which often would like to deal with very well defined areas during the interview and the time available is sharply defined.

All these interview models can be applied within one research project; the types of research previously cited were mostly indicative. Suppose you are using the opening-the-locks model to start asking what is involved in budgeting within families and in a next interview you examine some themes found with a tree-and-branches model. Suppose you find that it is women in particular, due to cultural perceptions on the role of women, who look after the budget. You might decide there and then to pursue those cultural perceptions – using the river model – because you think you cannot understand the budgeting within the nuclear family if you do not have an understanding deep enough of the position of women within this culture. However, this does not involve the cultural concepts regarding child rearing. Once the theme has been explored sufficiently, you turn back to the tree-and-branches model and the conversation guide you devised for it.

3.6   ELICITATION TECHNIQUES FOR INDIVIDUAL INTERVIEWS

Apart from formulating questions and responding to what is happening in inter-action with the respondent, some elicitation techniques might be considered when still planning the research. These often involve the use of specific stimuli when questioning respondents. Some examples are described in the following table.

Technique	Procedure	Examples
Sentence completion	The respondent is presented with half a sentence and asked to complete the sentence[a]	Jaffe (2005) used this technique in interviewing people in Jamaica and Curacao about their perceptions of residential neighbourhoods.
Participatory mapping	Respondents participate in drawing a consecutive series of maps relating to a specific theme or topic.	Van Est and Persoon (2000) used this technique in their future-oriented environmental research by asking respondents to draw a series of maps relating to land use.
Repertory grid[b]	Respondents are asked to choose two topics or themes from a triad that they think are similar and to explain the similarity. Next they are asked what could be the opposite choice.	Jaffe (2005) used this method in her research on perceptions of residential neighbourhoods in Curacao and Jamaica.
	This technique stems from market research. Respondents collect pictures or take photographs that express the meaning of a product for them. In several steps, the researcher tries to identify which images best represent the product and what they mean. The researcher creates a consensus chart based on individual opinions.	A description of this method can be found in De Ruyter & Scholl (2001)
Pilesort, based on a Freelist	This technique is intended to chart a cultural domain	Borgatti (1999) describes the procedure.
	Respondents are asked to name all elements relating to the domain in question (Freelist). Each element is then noted on a card and respondents are asked to make separate stacks of cards that name similar elements.	

[a] Johnson and Weller (2002) describe several variations of the type of categorization that Sentence completion and Repertory grid are looking for. Although they approach it in a very quantifying way and on the basis of assumptions that are certainly not always appropriate for qualitative research, it is useful to be aware of the existence of these techniques.
[b] This technique is sometimes referred to as Kelly grid (Vogel & Verhallen, 1983).

A very real danger in using such techniques is that the interview may be steered both by the selection of stimuli and the way in which these are introduced. Be aware of this and spend enough time on designing the stimuli you are going to apply and give thought to their potential impact.

3.7   CONVERSATION GUIDES

As has been raised earlier, there are different types of conversation guides one can develop. The checklist or interview guide with topics to discuss is the simplest format, a protocol with totally developed questions and sub-questions being the most extensive form. In-between the outline is a format, in which main questions function to inquire about themes, underpinned by more specific questions and maybe some specific examples the researcher wishes to explore. The topic list is a format used for a fairly heavily structured interview. Because of the dynamic structure of qualitative research the conversation guide might be adapted along the way. This type of preparation helps to strike a balance between the need for structure and the freedom to explore interesting themes (Laslett & Rapoport, 2003). Conversation guides need not be followed too rigidly; the natural tendency to structure the questions beforehand might dominate the conversation. Hollway and Jefferson (2003) describe nicely how they tried to move away from this tendency.

Preferably, a **conversation guide** would not be too lengthy. If a conversation guide takes up two pages or more, one might question whether this can be regarded a qualitative interview. To us, this is a semi-structured interview with open questions[7]. For an interview of 1-2 hours the appropriate conversation guide contains a maximum of six to eight main questions.

We choose to design our conversation guide prior to the interview because this enables us to give careful thought to an open wording without any underlying evaluative tone. Consequently, in our experience, the conversation guide is only needed as a reminder during the interview. In the interview itself we go along with what is happening. In most cases, we experienced that the themes on the conversation guide occur naturally to a large extent. Thus we only use the conversation guide as a starter at the beginning, en route when a subject is completed and at the end to check what has not been raised yet.

---

7. This form could be placed in-between qualitative and quantitative research. Its underlying attitude and thinking process leans more towards deductive reasoning than towards inductive or abductive reasoning.

3.8   WHAT KIND OF INTERVIEWER ARE YOU?

In Chapter 2, we discussed the various roles you might have as an interviewer. Before you reflect on what roles or style you – ideally – are about to adopt in your upcoming interview, you should first try to identify what type of individual you are. In Chapter 4 we will deal at length with **active listening**. Briefly speaking, it means the researcher is present in the interview with all his senses, which is the main condition for a good interview to happen. Active listening is not possible if he does not respect his own individuality. Going along with the respondent cannot succeed very well if he does not remain close to himself at the same time. Is his personality introvert, extrovert, does he respond mostly on second thoughts or does he have a ready tongue? Is there any personal baggage, e.g. painful experiences, which has prompted him to do this research? This kind of self-knowledge is an important determinant of how he functions in an interview. What might be his potential pitfalls[8] ? What are his strengths? He should enter an interview with respect for his individuality and at the same time try to avoid his pitfalls, i.e. the Skill. This implies that he often develops his own interview style, in which certain roles are better implemented than others. Because of the large degree of improvisation in an open interview, i.e. the Art, there is nothing against this. However, if he realizes that this sometimes has consequences for the kind of data he collects or their quality, he should ask himself what can be done to combat this.

It is important for you to investigate where your strengths lie because in practice you will often model your interviews according to your own strength. Conduct a trial interview with someone from your surroundings, tape it and listen to it on the basis of the checklist in the Appendix. Such self-knowledge can assist in designing a research project. Ideally, every researcher is supposed to design his research project according to the methodological optimum in which he chooses a method offering the best guarantee for the research question to be answered. In practice researchers have their own preferences and strengths which help determine their design. This seems worse than it actually is. It takes years of practice to be a good qualitative interviewer, just as it takes years of practice to design a good survey questionnaire. Even if you appreciate your preferences and strengths and have taken the time to train yourself in them, changing the Skill into an Art, it would still be wise to involve others for those parts where your strengths fall short. In this way the investigation will have an even greater chance of success.

---

8. Extrovert personalities may be more readily tempted to start talking about themselves during the interview. People investigating a subject that implies a painful memory to themselves, might become involved quite forcefully and may possibly be only able to 'see' the respondent through their own experience. People with a strong opinion about the research topic tend to reflect their own opinion about the issue through leading questions and thus influence the answers.

3.8.1   *The interviewer as a structuring mechanism: roles and styles*

In addition to the techniques already mentioned, e.g. interview model, question types and question content to structure the interview, the researcher's person or personality can also assist in structuring the interview. Krueger (1998), Van Fessem (personal communication) and our own experience inspired us to derive a number of roles and styles, which we elaborate on in greater detail below. Usually, the interviewer takes on several roles during an interview according to what the moment demands in his view. It is, therefore, advisable to be aware of all the possible roles you can take. These are:

Investigator: The researcher has a specific research goal and research question which constitutes the framework for the interview. Professionalism is required.

Director: The researcher is responsible for the smooth progress of the interview as well as a careful introduction and explanation of the research purpose and what will happen with the results. Another aspect of this role is ensuring the respondent feels heard and there is enough room for his story. This role can sometimes require expert navigating skills.

Summarizer: This role is not only used by the researcher to ensure he understood correctly what has been said but for closing a subject or steering the interview into another direction as well. At the end he summarizes the headlines of the entire interview in his own words to check whether something was left out. This requires much concentration during the whole interview and the ability to abstract away from what is said literally and look at it in a broader perspective.

Atmosphere maker: The interviewer ensures that a safe atmosphere is created in which respondents can talk about vulnerable aspects of themselves and have the courage to demonstrate these with examples. This requires much sensitivity and sometimes flexibility to respond to things that happen.

Teacher: Sometimes the interviewer needs to explain matters to respondents, e.g. the objective of the study or some abstract notions about which he would like to collect information. This requires a thorough preparation and the interviewer should have gained in-depth knowledge on his respondents beforehand to enable him to devise this explanation comprehensible. This role requires empathy.

Seeker/searcher: The interviewer is looking for the experiences or knowledge of the respondents and assumes that he is on track if he asks the right questions. This requires technical interview skills.

Detective: Additional to the seeker/searcher because people do not reveal everything, even though they are asked the right questions. Continued sensitivity to non-verbal signals and the atmosphere is required to find what they are – possibly – suppressing or hiding. This role requires unconditional presence of all the senses.

Linesman: This role supplements that of the researcher above: not only exactly knowing what he is looking for, but also being responsible for monitoring its boundaries. On the one hand, this means not cutting a possible interesting sideline too fast as he does not know what relevant information he might exclude. On the other hand, it means constantly asking himself whether information is still within the larger framework. This role requires much concentration.

Auto-monitor: The interviewer is constantly aware of himself and monitors whether he is properly conducting the interview, a role that requires much practice, self-reflection and a clear distinction between 'mine and thine' (Evers, 2003).

Challenger / schemer: The researcher sometimes uses a challenging question style because he believes the respondent is deliberately circumventing his questions or the answers are overly polished. Especially in policy-oriented, politically sensitive or other research involving many interests and sometimes with elites, this technique can be helpful. This requires careful wording[9], very good timing and a sense of atmosphere.

Timekeeper: If the researcher made an appointment for the interview based on a certain time estimate, it is of interest to monitor this especially for elites and when interviewing people in their workplace. On the other hand, if he notes signs of fatigue or loss of concentration on the part of either the respondent or him, that is a signal to stop the interview. Alertness to the outline of the interview is important, thus enhancing the chance of dealing with all his topics in the time available. This again requires navigation skills.

In addition to these desirable and sometimes necessary roles are the undesirable ones:

---

9. Especially in these situations it is particularly important to be able to articulate a neutral and an open question to which no opinion can be heard. People tend to suspect you have more sympathy for the other group and that puts pressure on your position. Be sure to be more alert of yourself in this type of intervention.

Commissioner: Respondents will sometimes see the interviewer as a representative of the person or organization who commissioned the research. It is important to properly explain the relationship, as well as what will happen with the results, which may or may not be anonymized.

Social worker: A situation can arise in an interview where respondents implicitly or explicitly ask for help which might range from a small favour, e.g. Could you please take out the garbage in leaving? to something that tends towards a dependency relationship. Where to draw the line is sometimes difficult to identify in advance. The researcher would best not put himself in the position of a 'saviour' or counsellor, as he is not. It might be better to point the respondent towards professional help.

Messenger: Sometimes respondents or commissioners would like to use the researcher as their messenger, either to protect their interests or to convey a painful message (Evers, 2003). Although qualitative research is aimed at giving respondents a 'voice' (Hertz, 1997) and make their voices heard, the researcher is not a messenger. It is up to the researcher to achieve valid results in the mix of voices, which sometimes all resemble different interests.

Companion: Respondents often ask the researcher for confirmation, while he at the same time identifies with their story, although to a differing extent. His role, however, is not that of a companion but of a researcher. Empathy can also be present without statements regarding one self. If he feels these are needed, he would preferably keep them for when the interview is finished.

3.9   PLANNING YOUR RESEARCH PROJECT

If permission is obtained for participation in the investigation, the interviews can be conducted. It is essential the method of recording and analyzing be known beforehand (cf. Chapter 7), as these may have an impact on the planning. Taking notes during an interview is a different matter if compared to taping the interview and transcribing it, which requires equipment and possibly the hiring of transcribers.

Conducting and transcribing interviews is a time-consuming business and it is important to plan sufficient time for both. Interviews should preferably be scheduled with sufficient time in-between, not only for the transcription, but also for the analysis. Furthermore, it is possible that after the analysis of each interview the researcher decides once again which type of respondent should preferably be interviewed next, such as to work on what is called 'theoretical sampling' (see Maso & Smaling, 2004: 37). Even if he is not planning theoretical sampling, it is better to plan sufficient intervals between interviews.

Number of interviews per day or week
We would advise to limit the number of open interviews per day to a maximum of two because firstly, the high level of concentration required during the interview absorbs a considerable amount of energy from the researcher. Secondly, he needs to process the information obtained before the next interview takes place. We usually plan at least half an hour – preferably an hour – of 'free time' before the start of an interview. This enables us to conduct the interview with full concentration without being preoccupied with other issues. It is, therefore, advisable to arrive at the place where the interview takes place in good time. It may also be necessary to plan 'free time' after the interview, especially if interviews are expected to probe quite deeply or become emotional because of the topic. That time is needed to process them, reflect about them and regain composure before starting the next interview. If the interviewer does not plan any time in between the first and the next interview, he runs the risk of not having 'freed' himself enough from the first respondent to enable him to listen to the next respondent with equal openness and empathy.

In a research project characterized by a cycle of data collection, analysis and reflection, which is followed by the same cycle of collection-analysis-reflection, the researcher might consider planning a maximum of eight interviews per month. This particularly applies to the early stages of the project, when a number of interviews can be conducted, analyzed, determined who the next respondent should be and whether the conversation guide and interview style is adequate. The number of interviews conducted per month can become higher in a subsequent period of the project, when possibly less time is required for analysis of the individual interviews. Thus in planning a project this way, in the first two months just a few interviews are conducted per month while in the next months this might increase to up to ten or twelve interviews per month.

In applied research, the data collection is often not followed by analysis immediately; all the interviews will usually be done first and transcribed, followed by a period of analysis. In this case it is advisable to build in some room for additional data collection.

How many interviews?

Usually a qualitative research project needs at least about twenty interviews to obtain a certain degree of saturation but opinions vary on this. The number of twenty is indicative for in-depth interviews on a certain subject, e.g. experience with sickness or undergoing a certain process. If the goal is a doctoral thesis in University, then at least thirty to forty interviews are needed. In market research, where interviews are much more structured and shorter and there is much less probing, the aim is usually a greater number than twenty interviews.

In other cases, for example in mapping an event that many and quite different persons have experienced in detail, e.g. the failure of a project in an organization with very serious implications, yet other numbers of interviews should be conducted.

This advice on planning applies to projects using open interviews which last about two hours. In research projects where interviews are more structured and shorter and are reported in a more summary form rather than a full verbatim transcription, more interviews per week or month can of course be planned.

It is difficult to prescribe a detailed planning of a research project using qualitative interviews, because the planning is quite dependent on the type of interview, the goal of the research project, the time available and the degree of experience the researcher has. However, the factors mentioned above might be taken into account in planning your project.

3.10   NO INTERVIEW WITHOUT PROPER PREPARATION

Despite the highly improvised nature of qualitative interviewing, we wish to stress the importance of proper preparation, both in designing the project and the interview questions, and thinking about the interview model, what is expected to happen at the content level and the roles one might adopt therein. Although in reality you often deviate from the questions formulated in advance, it does help if you have given some thought to how things can be formulated as openly and neutrally as possible. It is this thinking ahead that is used when improvising during the interview. The conversation guide[10], which was devised earlier is more of a memory aid and should not be treated as a rigid interview tool as we will see in Chapter 4. We recommend solid interview training as well in which questioning and improvising on what is happening is practised and in which feedback is received on actions and person(ality). You often come across differently from what you expect and a training course may help you gain greater insight. Interview training may prove equally useful at the start of a career and later on, after some years of experience: at the start to draw attention to how to go about interviewing, and later on to draw attention to ingrained patterns that may need some rectifying. You can also do much yourself to further develop your own interviewer skills. We have drawn up a checklist, cf. Appendix I, which might be used after each interview to reflect on its course and your own functioning therein. Benammar et al. (2006) illustrate a number of reflection methods, which might be applied.

---

10. A conversation guide is a list of topics or questions you make prior to the interview and which you take with you to the interview. The degree of preparation can vary greatly. See paragraph 2.5.3.

4 | Conducting an individual interview

Once the structure of the interview has been decided on, the appropriate aids[1] have been devised, i.e. interview guide, topic list, an opening question, etc., and appointments with respondents have been made, the interview can commence. In this chapter we will elaborate further on:

- Some techniques and types of question which can be used;
- The interviewers' attitude during the interview; and
- The organisational facts he must keep in mind.

Before we start with these, we would like to pause and draw your attention to an important skill for an interviewer: active listening.

4.1 THE IMPORTANCE OF ACTIVE LISTENING

The importance of **active listening** during a qualitative interview should not be under estimated. Active listening not only implies that you hear what is being said; you also need to put yourself in the position of your respondent, i.e. comprehend what he is saying and its possible implications to enable you to translate those back to your problem statement. We have termed this: thinking along analytically[2]. Trying to think along with a respondent explicitly does not imply putting words into his mouth. What it does mean is relating the non-verbal signals to the spoken information he provides. Active listening is also an expression of the interviewers' interest in the respondent's story.

---

1. Even though we emphasize the careful design of research, it is also important that during the design phase – once the interview type and target group is known – steps are taken to find and contact the target group. The recruitment phase takes a great deal of time; better not delay it for long.
2. By 'thinking along analytically' we mean that during the interview the information gathered is related to the problem statement, mutual relationships between items of obtained information are identified, the accuracy of these is checked with the respondent and it is assessed whether the information has been explored sufficiently deep to answer the question.

Listening: do you hear what the other is saying?
There are different ways of listening but sadly enough we are mostly poor listeners. The most familiar form of listening is receiving the message and responding immediately which is the form of communication we use in our daily lives. Answering is a signal the question has been received but it does not mean the question has been understood or will be answered. While conducting qualitative interviews, the researcher is doing much more than the kind of listening he does in his daily conversations. Asking questions and listening to the answer while interviewing involves four activities for the interviewer:
- Listening to the story without reacting immediately;
- 'Listening' with the eyes, i.e. looking at non-verbal signals in relation to the verbal message;
- Indicating verbally that he listens and observes by probing and regularly summarizing what was said by the respondent;
- Giving non-verbal signals that the story is being heard and seen, thus working on *rapport*;

While listening, the interviewer does not immediately react to the respondent. Instead he shows him that he is listening and that he is open to receive information. This can be done verbally, for example with a 'hm' or by saying 'yes', or he might summarise in his own words- at appropriate moments – what the respondent said to confirm that he understood it correctly, and probe on matters he would like to know more about. Non-verbally, he can show that he is open to what the respondent is saying by adopting an interested attitude. Looking at the respondent is important but it does not mean staring. The interviewer's attitude is calm and he does not pay much attention to other things, e.g. looking at his papers constantly, checking his watch, or fiddling. It helps if he sits with his back straight against the back of the chair[3] to maintain a relaxed attitude while giving the respondent enough room, i.e. not sitting 'on top' of him.

Listening is not a passive act. It demands a great deal of concentration because of the constant balancing between showing the respondent that you are thinking along and at the same time leaving enough room for his own direction. That is why it is not easy and extremely tiring: be sure you are well rested and conduct the interview with an 'empty' head. We usually make a point of having half an hour of 'empty' time prior to the interview and ensure we are present well ahead of the appointed time. Then, we emphatically focus on emptying our minds of daily concerns but also of expectations concerning the interview.
In listening, the interviewer keeps three goals in mind: understanding the information, evaluating it with regard to his interview goal and monitoring the –

---

3. 'Keep your bottom in the chair!' is an expression we heard from an actor during a role-play. For us it demonstrates the point explicitly.

emotional – status of the respondent to check whether he is showing sufficient empathy and interest.

On the one hand, he follows the story of the respondent while showing him that he understands. On the other hand, he interprets the information received in relation to his problem statement and checks the accuracy of it by summarizing regularly. He also assesses whether this is enough and whether it answers his question and reacts with a follow-up question. Conclusively: this is a *high-order mental process* (Gorden, 1998:82) and definitely not an automatism.

The difficulty lies in being able to process the incoming information without losing the concentration needed to continue listening. If the researcher is thinking about his next action, about identifying relations between the information obtained and the problem statement, or about his own presumptions concerning the research, he often no longer listens to the respondent. He is busier organizing the information obtained and thinking about his reaction. Thus, he can only 'think along analytically' on a limited scale, as all this has to happen in a split second. The real analysis, in his reflective memos and during the analysis of the transcript, takes place at a later stage, after having conducted the interview.

The second aspect that makes it difficult to combine listening and ordering information is that the interviewer does not know beforehand what information he will receive. Probably, the information is new to him as well which results in him not always having the verbal resources at hand to react adequately. In such cases he might choose to limit himself to summarizing and probing to ensure depth and better understanding and leave the analytical relations for a later stage when he knows more. The active listener might also become overly active and interrupt the respondent too often in his story. Not only does this behaviour interrupt the flow of the interview, it also often means he becomes too directing. He thus might miss interesting information and might even irritate the respondent and lose his *rapport*.

Physical circumstances can also make listening more difficult: noise, distracting behaviour by the respondent, presence of a third party at the interview, poor enunciation on the part of the respondent or fatigue or poor hearing on the part of the interviewer. There can also be semantic obstacles: dialect, the usage of certain words with a specific connotation, for example, job related jargon or cultural connotations. There can also be emotional barriers: lack of interest in the subject on the part of either interviewer or respondent, bias on the part of either party causing failure to hear what is being said, strong reactions to loaded words, self-referential statements by the interviewer and fear of the interviewer of losing control over the interview.

4.2   APPLYING DIFFERENT TYPES OF QUESTIONS

In the following paragraph we look at the various types of questions which might be used during the interview. We start with main questions.

4.2.1   *Main questions*

In Chapter 3 we discussed how the chief role of main questions is to structure the interview in the direction of the problem statement. The key factor in designing the main questions is to ensure that they address the themes earlier established as of apparent relevance to the stated problem. This is quite separate from the form in which these themes are going to be shaped for the interview, i.e. the opening-the-locks model, the river model or the tree-and-branches model. The distilled main question used as an opening question within the opening-the-locks model or the river model, or the main questions that are going to be identified in the conversation guide in using the tree-and-branches model, should be examined in terms of the degree to which they embrace the entire problem statement.

When using a **conversation guide**, the interviewer should ensure that the questions overlap smoothly so that the respondent might experience them as meaningful. For example, when the point is to reconstruct an experience the main questions should be in a chronological order. He ought to check whether the questions in his conversation guide are consistent with the intention of the problem statement, i.e. pay attention to specific definitions of concepts, and ensure they are operationalized adequately in the interview questions. These might be fine-tuned in the course of the project. Keep the number of main questions limited; a maximum of six to eight questions per interview ensures that sufficient richness and depth is obtained.[4] Although this might not seem many questions, you will be probing as well or use other ways to continue talking. This implies that much information per question can be obtained and that is why often the conversation guide is put aside after the first question. If everything goes according to plan, the interview takes its own course and the conversation guide is no longer needed. This enhances the spontaneous proceeding of the interview. If the interviewer is constantly checking his conversation guide, the interview becomes more of a question-and-answer session, thus interrupting the **flow** of it. Possibly not all of the questions can be addressed or the respondent might address other themes in relation to the problem statement than had previously occurred to the researcher. In such a case, our advice is to remain flexible. Themes that have not been covered but seem important can resurface in the next interview. However, when conducting evaluation research or when clarifying a specific event or process it is important that all questions are asked.

---

4.   We assume a maximum interview time of approximately two hours.

The themes the researcher would like to cover during a **thematic interview** are transposed into a series of questioning lines which together cover the different phases of a specific event or of a process. In a **cultural interview** this represents only a source of help in inspiring the respondent to start talking about his particular culture or important issues of his daily life. Most of the work is in probing and asking follow-up questions and here active listening is the most important technique for deciding what is potentially interesting to probe into further. This requires a high level of concentration. A main question in a cultural interview is formulated in such a way that it invites the respondent to describe his daily routine, or the facts concerning the area in which the interviewer is interested in, in everyday language. For example: 'Could you tell me what kind of a day you had yesterday?' Or: ' I would like to know how you interact. Could you tell me how to become a member of your group?' And a probe: Who cannot become a member? What makes somebody a group member? When are you excluded? Where do you meet? Probe: What happens when you are together, what do you do, how do you make an appointment?

Conclusion
In formulating his main questions, the researcher pays attention to:
- **Scope**: the question should make clear which subject or domain will be the focus of the interview. Within that domain, the specific interest is in the perception or experience of the respondent[5] ;
- **Steering**: the question is stated broadly enough to disguise the specific focal points, assumptions or hypotheses that the researcher has formulated to himself beforehand;
- **Level of abstraction**: the question is worded in such concrete and everyday language that the respondent can answer it[6].

Once every main question has been explored properly, it can be useful to finalise by briefly summarising each question and answer. The respondent is thus given an overview and the chance to see whether anything has been left out. The interviewer then moves on to the next question (Maso as cited in Kuijlman & Bos, 2003).

---

5. Take care to stick with this experience during the interview. We call this 'empirical reference' (cf. Baart, 2002:4, 16-17). The point is that the respondent relates what he or she has experienced, and not what others experienced according to him or her.
6. In our educational context we often encounter questions that are too academic/intellectual/abstract, so that the respondent has no idea what is asked. Make sure to adapt your use of language to that of the respondent – a bricklayer's use of language differs from that of a company executive – and remember: written language differs from spoken language. It helps to first read your questions out loud, or try them on friend or colleagues, other acquaintances, the greengrocer or your local supermarket.

4.2.2   *Verbal and non-verbal probing*

As noted in Chapter 3, probing is used to bring more depth into a theme and flow into the interview. The interviewer thereby asks for more details without changing the subject. By constantly referring back to the experience of the respondent, i.e. the **empirical reference**, he focuses on both depth and –to a lesser extent – width to get a picture, which is both complete and valid and adds to the reliability of the project as well. In asking for empirical references the interviewer might use the four aspects mentioned by Baart (2002: 16-17) to frame his question. These are: a) Indications: can the respondent cite examples?, b) Situations: where/when or with whom does this happen?, c) Conditions: when is it called for?, and d) Analysis: what are the respondent's thoughts on this?

In probing, the interviewer notes the **body language** of the respondent. If he picks up non-verbal signals, he should ask about these. They could be signals related to the story being told, cf. the table below, as well as signals that contradict what is being said.

Sometimes in probing, the interviewer can **add elements** known to him or assumptions he has. Assessing what might be added in a question and what not is fairly complicated. A rule of thumb might be to treat a respondent as a partner in conversation. If you are aware that people who practise certain meditation methods experience fatigue as a side effect but the respondent has not mentioned this as yet, you could check on this with an open question. This not only requires a great deal of practice but also self-reflection after every interview, cf. the Art and Skill.

It is important to **refrain from steering** the interview through probing if possible. Questions which are formulated in a suggestive or evaluative manner, throw doubt on the validity of collected data and thus on the entire research project. For this reason, the interviewer formulates open questions and avoids using suggestive or evaluative words. Some probes might already be designed together with the conversation guide. Examples can be found in Schensul, Schensul and LeCompte (1999:127-128). Some standard expressions and neutrally formulated probes can be found in the table below.

Table 4.1   Verbal and non-verbal probing techniques

Verbal	Example	Non-verbal	Example
Stimulate/invite[a]	Hummmm, 'yes yes' or saying okay, with a neutral or questioning tone. Tone is important, as this can be seen as an internal agreement.	Stimulating/inviting	Nodding, look at the respondent invitingly; lean forward in your chair every now and then.
Repeat the question[b], but not literally	Okay, I was curious about what you like about your job. Could you tell me something about this?	Listening It is important to let the respondent notice that you are listening.	By regularly looking at the respondent you signal that you are interested. This can be done through you glance, i.e. inviting, questioning, and in your body language, i.e. calm, leaning back and sometimes slightly moving forward.
Clarify your question[c]	I would like to know what you like about your job. You mentioned working part-time. Are there any more aspects?	Clarify your question	A questioning glance, leaning a bit towards the respondent.
Echoing Repeat part of the answer of the respondent in a questioning tone.	The thing you like most is that your job is part-time? Am I correct in assuming this?	Silence, let something pass for a few moments. Silent moments offer room for organizing the mind, they invite the respondent to say more and allow for a moment's rest in the interview.	If a respondent remains silent, you have the tendency to fill up this silence. But sometimes the respondent is gathering his or her thoughts; a question from the interviewer might disrupt this process. Inviting glance.
Un-aimed explicit probes i.e. direct and/or retrospective elaboration	What do you mean? Could you elaborate a bit more? Could you tell me some more about it? How did you find out? I can see this is a sensitive subject for you, would you like to talk about it? Here, it is suitable to remain silent[d] for a while.	Adjust to your respondent Make it clear through the use of your body language that you are listening and that you pick up non-verbal signals.	If the respondent says something that seems difficult to him, lean backwards and show him through your body language that there is room for change of tempo and choices. Show empathy through your glance.

Verbal	Example	Non-verbal	Example
Aimed explicit probes or confronting probes[e] i.e. direct or retrospective clarification	That is how it started; how did it proceed? You mentioned earlier not choosing this option. It seems to me you did choose for it in this case, or do I misunderstand you? What do you think about that? I understood that Polish workers are being used as well. Do you have any experience with this? What happened next?		
Summarising The interviewer summarises the core of what was said and presents this to the respondent. This technique can be applied while probing, to keep track if overloaded with information, to check whether he understood correctly, or to finalise a topic.	If I understand you correctly, you like having a part-time job. It gives you more time to do other things such as working out, going out and staying in touch with your family. You often babysit your brother's children. Have I summarised this correctly?		
Explaining by using a fictive situation For example when confronted with a difficult technical story.	If you would have to explain to somebody who never read about this or has never been there, how would you do this?		
After a generalisation or oversimplification	You say that this only happens with foreign patients. Is this so with all of your foreign patients?		

[a] This technique works invitingly and adds to the *rapport*.

[b] Do not apply this technique too often as it can become irritating.

[c] Be careful with this technique as your own interpretation or assumptions might sneak in easily.

[d] By 'confronting' we mean that you mention perceptible contradictions in the story of the respondent or confront the respondent with contradictory or controversial information in your possession relating to the subject

[e] Here, you react to the non-verbal signals of the respondent, his or her body language. A good rule of thumb for the researcher is, if the respondent reacts emotionally – whether or not predictable, to react from an empathetic attitude and not mere curiosity, i.e. voyeurism (see Smaling, 2007). Of course, the interests of the research play an underlying role here too, but we believe its importance should be secondary to that of the respondent. What does he need? Show your willingness to talk about emotions, but allow him to refrain from doing so. Guard against the pitfall of acting like a social worker, which you are not. If the respondent is in need of help, be sure to advise him where to go for support.

Pay attention to just use probes selectively and not automatically, as this affects respondents negatively. Do not probe too often either, as it interrupts the flow of the interview and might be irritating.

4.2.3   *Verbal follow up questions*

As discussed earlier in Chapter 2, follow-up questions address new themes that were introduced by the respondent. These questions always stem from the respondent's answers to the main questions. They can be regarded as main questions on second instance; they fine tune the problem statement and lead to the actual understanding of the problem being explored. Some of the follow-up questions are formulated during interim analysis, while others surface during the actual interview. Whatever the case, follow-up questions need to be considered in between interviews and certainly after each cluster of interviews. Formulating follow-up questions during the interview, while listening actively to the respondent, is difficult and requires much training. The skill lies in formulating only those follow-up questions that might offer insight into the core problem statement. This raises the importance of giving the design considerable thought beforehand which will enable the researcher to formulate adequate follow-up questions during the interview. Here, Art follows Skills.

The following points may help identify potential themes for follow-up questions. Some points are indicative of a follow-up question, others require initiative by the interviewer:
• Unilateral description of behaviour;
• Contradictions in the story
• Approaching the subject from contrasting points of view;
• Asking the respondent for the opposite of what he or she is saying;
• Issues the interviewer thinks absolutely astonishing.

These are only a few suggestions that can help formulate a follow-up question. They often only relate to gaps in the information. Some subjects are clearly candidates for follow-up questions, while others are more subtle and less immediately obvious. In the latter case, this might only occur to the interviewer as needing more in-depth examination a couple of interviews later, for example during the analysis of the transcripts. If a considerable number of themes surface as candidates for follow-up questions, the researcher might sketch clusters of questions surrounding multiple themes as questioning lines to pursue. Ideas that occur while doing this are noted consecutively in a memo or research logbook[7]. During the interviews he indicates which themes have already been dealt with, thus tracking the progress of the interview endeavour.

When framing and asking follow-up questions it is advisable to keep the following points in mind:
- Follow-up questions should remain close to what the respondent has just said and not suddenly broach a new subject (cf. Booth & Booth, 2003). The interviewer might link two issues mentioned by the respondent and ask whether these are related.
- Start follow-up questions with an empirical reference to the respondent's own life or his experience. If the interviewer starts questioning general themes the respondent might respond in generalisations without reference to the impact of the theme on his own life or experience.
- Before using follow-up questions designed beforehand and based on previous interviews, ensure they are still relevant to the current story being told by the respondent. If not, adapt the question.

It is better not to use follow-up questions if the respondent is putting up a front, or account (Rubin & Rubin, 2005:138) or if there is resistance of some sort (Stroeken, 2000:30). A **front**, the term comes from Goffman, is when somebody is trying to emphasize his image by exaggerating his role. An **account** is when somebody is offering self-defensive explanations for unacceptable behaviour, thus hoping to make it socially acceptable. **Resistance** denotes that the respondent is reluctant to be present or to participate in the interview. This will generally be expressed in the form of muttered phrases or minor behavioural gestures. Stroeken recommends talking about resistance before proceeding with the interview. Of course, resistance can be displayed right from the onset of the interview. If so, do not ignore it but discuss it.

Overlap between probing and follow-up questions
It is not always possible to distinguish clearly between probing and follow-up questions; they may sometimes intertwine during the interview[8]. It is sometimes difficult to separate them because they complement each other and might have overlapping functions, notably when:

---

7. If QDA software is used to support a project, e.g. Atlas.ti, MaxQDA, NVivo, or Kwalitan, we assume the progress of the project and the development of thoughts surrounding it have been recorded in memos. To enhance the reliability of the project and work more systematically we advise you to use QDA software from the start of the project.
8. The same applies to the term *content mining questions*, used by Legard, Keegan and Ward (2004: 148). These questions, although intended to bring depth into the interview following explorative questions asked earlier, i.e. *content mapping questions*, are in their form either probes or follow-up questions.

- The interviewer would like broad information: he would like to identify the different facets of a subject. The positive side, but the negative too. It was a clear choice or there was no choice.
- He would like to explore the nuances of a subject in-depth: for example shades of meaning when something is explained as being unpleasant. What is considered unpleasant? When is something less unpleasant?
- He would like to gain a deeper understanding of a subject, for example understand the nature of an experience: how important is this in the life of the respondent and what determines the degree of importance attached to it? What does the respondent mean in saying something is unpleasant and what meaning is attached to the different shades of it?
- He is monitoring the validity of the data presented, e.g. asks questions about inconsistencies: 'you mentioned that ... but later... Could you elaborate on this?

Despite the overlap, we think it illuminating to retain the distinction between the two types of questions. However, it is important the interviewer carefully builds a line of questioning during the interview. He might start with clarifying questions before asking questions that might be embarrassing or confrontational. For example, he starts with 'facts': What happened?, then moves on to perception: What did you think about that?, followed by feeling: How did that affect you? If the respondent follows his line of questioning with sufficient depth, he can put his prepared follow-up questions aside for the moment and proceed with probing until he decides to address a following theme.

To encourage recalling topics the interviewer wishes to probe into or follow-up later, he might note them as **keywords**[9] during the interview. Preferably, he uses the words of the respondent, as these will be easiest for him to recall later on. However, this may prompt a learning effect: the respondent may become increasingly better at assessing what type of information he is seeking and may anticipate on that in his responses. This is sometimes seen as an advantage, as it helps to interview more time-efficiently (Rubin & Rubin 2005). However, we would like to point out that it may also be a disadvantage because the respondent may become overly selective or selective in the wrong direction. He should, therefore, try to keep an open mind, listen actively, and keep his selection of possible interesting topics within the framework of his problem statement. This requires a great deal of concentration and fairly good analytical ability to assess those topics rapidly, as well as the ability to distinguish what is the respondent's reaction and what could be the interviewer's input or bias. You might want to train yourself in this ability.

---

9. We assume that you always tape an interview; for that reason we speak of jotting down keywords instead of taking extensive notes.

Table 4.2   **Situations in which probes and follow-up questions are appropriate**

Situation	Example
If you would like more information on a situation, possibly preceded by a summary.	You said that you cried a lot when your father died and you stayed away from school for two weeks. Was there somebody around to talk with you about the death of your father?
Following a generalization or oversimplification	You told me that you strongly feel that you are not understood. Can you tell why you feel that way?
	You said you always work until six because of your appointments. Is the end of your working day determined by your appointments?
If a respondent unexpectedly introduces something new or something you have not heard before	You said it was not planned. What do you mean by 'not planned', could you explain?
If the respondent has mentioned something earlier which is of interest to you and you come back to it later	You said earlier that you sometimes 'let the day unravel itself'. Can you tell me more? When did you last let the day unravel itself?
Asking for further explanation if information is contradictory	Earlier you mentioned that your working day is always fully planned. You mentioned as well that you sometimes let the day unravel itself. Can you tell me what is the difference between the two?
Challenge the respondent to give you more information or explain contradictory information	Do you think your ethnic background makes you feel this way?
	You said you always plan the whole of your working day and you said that you let the day unravel itself. This seems contradictory to me, can you explain?
Break through the formal level of conversation. This technique is specifically appropriate in interviewing respondents in their professional capacity or people who find it hard to identify their own perceptions or feelings	I've heard of this approach several times before, but I'm curious about your side of the story. How do *you* see this policy?
	What I would really like to find out is how this behaviour of your daughter affects *you*?
If certain information is not mentioned while you are quite sure that it applies to comparable situations	We talked about the side effects you had from chemotherapy and you did not mention fatigue. Could you elaborate on that?

In the interview, various types of questions overlap, although this happens less with main questions in comparison to probes and follow-up questions. Main questions need not necessarily be used in the chronological order the researcher had planned earlier. Be flexible about that and adapt to the pace of the respondent. This is one of the ways to use your Skill in order to attain the Art of interviewing. It will help bring flow into the interview and promote *rapport*. The respondent feels he is being accepted for what he is.

4.3   PATTERNS OF INTERACTION DURING A QUALITATIVE INTERVIEW

Aside from the various types of questions discussed above, other aspects of the interaction between the interviewer and the respondent affect the quality of the data. We discuss these in the following paragraphs.

4.3.1   Behaviour of interviewer and respondent

The importance of **continuous observation** of the respondent is – in our opinion – the prime concern. Observing the respondent during the interview provides indications on subjects for further exploration, subjects the respondent might be hiding, and possible contradictions between what he is saying and what his body language seems to communicate. Ensure to do this unobtrusively, otherwise it can be counterproductive. These observations ought to be used, either as probes or follow-up questions. Remember, however, that you are not the only one observing; the respondent is observing you in turn. He is also trying to read your body language in order to decipher whether he gives the right answers and whether they meet your expectations.

There is something else at play as well which has been termed transfer and counter-transfer: people generate emotions in each another which influences their conscious or unconscious reactions to each other. Stroeken (2000: 32-39) comments on this phenomenon: 'We people seldom or never have a direct meeting with each other. People always speak to absentees, to people of whose presence we are unaware. People often do not speak 'face to face', but 'imagination to imagination'.'(2000: 33. Transl. by JE). Stroeken thus indicates that people arouse unconscious associations about other people from your past, and that those associations determine your present reaction, at least in part. This undercurrent in the contact between two persons is on a relational level and as such might not be in accordance with the content of what is being communicated or with the research aim.

The following paragraphs give a number of examples of behaviour by either the respondent or the interviewer, which may damage the information obtained or interfere with the flow of the interview.

4.3.2   Behaviour of the respondent

Some respondents are **inconsistent** in their responses; be attentive to this. It might mean the interviewer has misunderstood something but it may also mean the respondent might have liked to conceal or embroider something and had a slip of the tongue, in which case it is a validity problem. It is best to assume initially that there has been no inconsistency but a misunderstanding on your part, as this is frequently the case.

It is difficult to raise these inconsistencies without giving the respondent the feeling that he is caught mistaken. Try to question this in an open way without referring to the inconsistency and without being evaluative. An example: the respondent has told you he always goes to church on Sundays. When talking about his activities on the last two Sundays he appeared to have been doing other things. First, you might want to check if your data are correct: 'You said you always go to church on Sunday?' and at a quite different point in the interview, for example, if you check the activities of the last two weeks again: 'Did you go to church those Sundays?' What matters is that you try to prevent the respondents feeling attacked and becoming defensive. This might make them circumvent your question and make excuses.

When a **respondent diverges** from the topic in a way that the interviewer thinks irrelevant to the problem statement, it might be a sign that he does not fully understand what the respondent would like to say. He might resolve such a situation by referring back to the problem statement without mentioning the divergence. An example: the problem statement concerns the motivation of people to meditate. The respondent begins to describe methods she uses to calm herself, citing all sorts of things: knitting, reading books, hiking, anything but meditation. The interviewer might then ask how the respondent defines meditation or a meditative activity and if she has done so, ask whether she regards all those other things she mentioned, i.e. knitting, reading books, hiking, as a meditative activity.

It is important that the interviewer considers actively whether matters mentioned by the respondent are perhaps unintentional answers to his problem statement or that the respondent has diverged from the topic because

- She cannot answer the question because she does not understand it. See whether reformulating the question helps;
- She cannot transpose your question to apply to her own life; this applies mainly to abstract problem statements such as: what are moral moments in the working life of mental health carers? How important in the work of medical specialists is it to give meaning to life? and so on. It helps to return to the problem statement and check whether it was sufficiently operationalized by reformulating the main question;
- She refuses to answer that question. Stress that she is at liberty to decide whether or not to answer all the questions posed.

Sometimes a researcher encounters respondents who keep **talking incessantly** and sometimes about matters unrelated to the subject. These non-stop talkers are difficult to curb; the interviewer might try using intervening summaries to bring the respondent back to the subject. This does not always work and he simply cannot get a word in between. He might then try to gain control again by using short interpolative sentences, repeating words the respondent has just mentioned:

'I would like to return to … ' or: ' Why did you not join?' If that is unsuccessful as well, he might introduce the point that he has a number of questions he would like to ask. In general, we recommend that you first just wait and see. Perhaps the respondent only needs to get something off their chest before they have room for the interview. If after a while – about fifteen minutes to half an hour – you are convinced you have a true case of non-stop talking, you can then try the above strategies.

Another type of behaviour sometimes found in respondents, is the so-called '**oyster**': someone who replies only with a yes or no and can scarcely be persuaded to elaborate further. This too can be extremely difficult. First, the interviewer might try to reformulate his queries into open, inviting questions: Can you tell me more about that? Could I ask you to describe an example? If this does not help, he might emphasise the fact that he is really interested in what the respondent has to say, however trivial it might seem to him. If this is still ineffective, then he might bring it out into the open. He might mention being under the impression the respondent finds it difficult or annoying to answer his questions and ask them for the reason.

Some respondents have a tendency to answer every question with a **counter question**. In such cases, make clear right away that the interview is not about you but about them and that you are only interested in – the world of – the respondent. If the counter questions aim at getting to know you in the context of building up rapport, you could indicate that you are willing to deal with that after the interview has ended.

To conclude the possible respondent behaviours, we would like to mention the **strategic respondent** who evades all the questions he is unwilling to answer. This often happens in research where many interests are involved. It is important to start working on rapport from the start, giving the respondent confidence that the interviewer will carefully handle the information received. The interviewer might try to breach the barrier by asking about his or her perception of the case at hand. This will sometimes not work. He might then try a more challenging approach which might involve having to resort to a loaded or evaluative proposition, followed by an open question. For example: the respondent has just made an impressive speech about how well his organization is doing. You probe by stating the following: 'Well that is a really great story. Often there is a story for the outside world and an internal story how things are really doing. How is that in your organization?'

4.3.3   *Behaviour of the interviewer*

Sometimes it is advised to ask the respondent for permission to **quote him** on a specific point (Rubin & Rubin 2005). In our view this is not useful in an interview situation; it might act as a deterrent and influence the atmosphere negatively, while at that point it is not yet clear whether this quotation would ever be used in the research report. A better option would be to wait until the analysis is complete. If it appears later that using certain quotes might be problematic because people may have said things off the record or because the researcher cannot readily assess how recognizable the respondent is to others and whether this could possibly have repercussions for him, he might ask permission for the quotes he is certain he really would like to use. This will usually only apply to research projects involving many interests or where individuals are easily recognisable. In other circumstances it is not necessary to ask respondents for their permission to quote.

Referring to another – fictitious – respondent when posing a question (Maso & Smaling, 2004) is a strategy to be adopted only with the greatest circumspection. It demands great awareness from the respondent of the consequences of a question, the assertiveness to dissociate himself if necessary, and the capability of putting this directly into words. Not everyone has this ability[10]. If the researcher really would like to ask something because he has observed it in other respondents, he could still formulate it in such a way that it does not refer to other persons. We recommend keeping the question open and regarding the respondent himself. An example: 'You have just told me about the symptoms you are having because of this disease and mentioned among other things insomnia and feelings of unrest.' Others have told you and literature mentions that people always suffer from stinging legs and constipation as well. You might translate this knowledge into a probe: 'Do you suffer from anything else that you think may be related to this disease?'

The same caution applies to **conclusive sentences** in which the interviewer adds his own interpretation: 'So in your view, before your partner died he was not available to you either? So that was the only important thing your husband did? ' (Maso & Smaling, 2004: 90). In our view it is better to keep such assumptions to yourself: 'I understand that … Is this true, am I right in thinking that?' or a very open question: 'What do you mean by that?'

_____

10. People who are assertive and verbally uninhibited or accustomed to being in charge or to dealing
    with the media will probably have no difficulty in doing this.

4.4   IN WHICH WAY WILL YOU STRUCTURE YOUR INTERVIEW?

In Chapter 3, we dealt at length with ways of structuring the interview in paragraph 3.5, the use of elicitation techniques in paragraph 3.6 and conversation
guides in paragraph 3.7. Since we have already discussed the question types and
interaction patterns that occur during an interview, this is a good time to remind
you of the mechanisms and means of structuring. In the table below we have
combined interview models with interview types. We have rated how appropriate a model is to a specific interview type with pluses (++). Certain interviewer
roles will be applicable to more or less any combination of interview model and
type.

Table 4.3   Interview models versus interview types

	Interview model		
Interview type	*Opening the locks*	*River*	*Tree and branches*
Cultural	+++	++	+
Thematic	+	++	+++

From the table above it is clear that all interview models may be applied to both
types of interviews but that they are not always equally adequate. Almost all the
interviewer roles discussed in Chapter 3 will be applicable but in varying degrees. In particular the roles of teacher, linesman, challenger and time watch are
not always necessary.
How matters are combined will not only depend on the time available for the research project but especially on the phase it is in. If the tree-and-branches model
does not immediately seem appropriate for a cultural interview, it could still be a
very appropriate style in the final phase of a project. Equally, the opening-the-
locks model may be more appropriate at the start of a thematic interview than
for any of the other styles. So experiment with these and reflect on the impact of
the one versus the other. Your personal strengths as an interviewer are undoubtedly relevant here as well. So include these in your consideration and reflection.

4.5   POINTS OF INTEREST IN CONDUCTING INDIVIDUAL INTERVIEWS

In the preceding paragraphs we focused on the techniques and methods which
can be applied in a qualitative interview. In this paragraph the person(ality) of
the interviewer in such interviews and the relationship he develops with the respondent are discussed. These two aspects specifically determine the flow of the
interview. Can you listen carefully? Do you truly hear what the respondent is
saying? Can you set aside your own bias and the theoretical framework of your

research project[11] and respond to what is happening? We believe techniques are above all necessary tools to ensure the interview runs smoothly. The *real* quality of the interview is determined by the extent to which you create enough space for the respondent to be himself, while keeping the interview within the framework of the problem statement *and* at the same time trying to create a maximum of space to explore its boundaries. It is thus no coincidence that the title of this book refers to qualitative interviewing as Art *and* Skill.

In Chapter 3 the roles the interviewer can deploy during the interview were described in detail. Besides those roles the interviewer has different tasks while his attitude, which sometimes overlaps with his role, is important for the development of sufficient rapport. In this paragraph, all of this will be discussed in detail.

First, the distinction between the dimensions of empathy and distance in the relationship between the interviewer and the respondent are discussed. Navigating between these two poles while in contact with respondents can sometimes be quite difficult. We have slightly amended the distinction as defined by Baart (2002) and describe both poles below:

Empathy, i.e. putting yourself in the shoes of the other, includes:
1. Understanding: you hear facts and feelings of the respondent and describe these;
2. Proximity: you are meticulous, listen actively, pick up signals, have an appropriate attitude, sometimes help to articulate[12] and reassure where appropriate;
3. Respect: you do not make qualifying statements, you react with respect, stimulate, suspend assessments on matters even if the respondent asks, and remain in the background yourself;
4. Fairness: you are correct about the aim of your questions, behave consistently, speak only for yourself, you do not accept gifts which cannot be accounted for, if necessary you separate out conversational sequences, i.e. during and after the interview.

---

11. Theoretical framework to our mind is the preparatory literature review, conducted to enable you to design your research project. Generally, you will distill a conceptual model from the literature in which you describe the relationships between the main concepts with regard to your subject of interest.
12. Aid in articulating is appropriate if people are having trouble finding the core of what they would like to express. You can help them by using probes to return their stories in concepts which you believe reflect the essence of what they are saying and verifying whether that was what they meant. However, be careful in doing this and stress that the interpretation is yours only and may very well be incorrect because you can quite readily put words into their mouths.

Distance, i.e. keeping your distance towards the other, includes:
1. Intellectual virtues: you are inquisitive, you stay in the background, you have genuine interest, openness and intellectual naïveté;
2. Critical weighing of replies: you ask for clarification, supplement, detail and specification, you may submit a hypothesis that occurs to you based on what was said and offer your interpretations expressly as being yours;
3. You guide the interview with a soft touch when possible, and a stronger emphasis where appropriate[13], i.e. you are both social-emotional and task oriented.

Finally, some authors discuss sharing your own uncertainties and feelings about the interview with respondents (e.g. Maso & Smaling, 2004). We would make a subtle distinction between technical and relational uncertainties. In our opinion, **uncertainties** on a technical level, i.e. the methods and techniques used; the how of the investigation, can best be shared with fellow researchers. Relational uncertainties require a different approach. A good rule of thumb is perhaps to let the human side of the relationship with the respondent guide your approach. There is no harm in asking a respondent how he has experienced the interview, or whether he feels sufficiently heard. The interviewer might also express his gratitude to the respondent; for their time and the provision of information which can sometimes be an emotional burden. If his functioning as an interviewer is below par during the interview due to internal causes[14] he can mention this briefly and if his concentration does not return fast enough, he may prefer to break off the interview. Afterwards, when pondering on the incident, possibly aided by a colleague, he might try to identify what went wrong and possibly discuss it with the respondent in a later phase. If his work is hampered by external factors: the respondent does not seem willing to cooperate, he is constantly disturbed by third parties etc., he might want to mention this at some point. However, it is advisable to do this in an open, enquiring manner and leave it to the respondent to decide whether or not to end the interview and continue it another time.

We have combined the above mentioned aspects of both the attitude and tasks of the interviewer in a table.

---

13. Although we strongly recommend an with a minimum of steering, we sometimes have to guide the interview more than we ideally wish, based on a timeframe. We firmly believe this can still be done with a soft touch. Some respondents are readily inclined to sidetrack or to constantly repeat themselves. In that case you have to sometimes nudge the respondent in the right direction with a slightly more dominant touch.
14. By internal causes we mean affairs which primarily belong to your responsibility/personality, such as: you think the respondent is very attractive, you went to a party yesterday and it was a late night, you are somewhere else in your mind, you have an acute aversion of the respondent, etc.

Table 4.4   Tasks and attitude of the interviewer during an interview

Tasks	How	Attitude	How
Introduction of the interview	You provide background information on the research project[a], data processing, ask permission to tape the interview and promise confidentiality[b], you ensure the logistics are in order, i.e. extra batteries, your voice recorder is working and is ready, paper and pencil are at hand, mobile phone is switched off.	You put the respondent at ease	Exude calmness, explain the purpose of the interview, make room for questions, do not sit opposite to the respondent, do not perch at the edge of your chair but rest your back in the seat, but not too relaxed.
Influence the interview situation as to ensure enough room for the exchange of information	Try to ensure the interview can be held in a quiet room[c], be flexible about external interferences: telephone, noise, interruption, and internal disturbances: wrong respondent, there is strong aversion or too much attraction between the two of you, you do not get relevant information.	Accept what happens, exude comprehension and intervene only if things really exceed your limits	Exude tranquillity, do not get off track, and stay focused on your interview goal without letting this ruin the relationship. If an interference, either internal or external is too much, propose to move the interview to another time or talk about it.
Ask your questions	Do your best to refrain from influencing the respondent in formulating his answer.	Listen attentively and actively, show that you have time for this interview, only jot down keywords	Make eye contact regularly, nod your head or hum, let silences fall for a while, summarize what you hear, probe if you do not understand or would like to know more about something, present relations you see between statements in an open way, refrain from 'self-announcements' or evaluative comments[d]
Evaluate given answers	• Valid: do the actions, feelings and thoughts described by the respondent correspond to your questions? • Exhaustive: have you heard everything there is to hear? • Relevant: has your question been answered?	Ensure when you probe into inconsistencies that you do this in a neutral formulation. Check your interpretation of answers with the respondent.	Present matters as your own interpretation: I understood this to be such at first, and now I understand it to be so. Am I correct in assuming this?
Keep track of your line of questioning	Note issues you would like to address later on in keywords.	Ensure eye contact	Do not look at your papers constantly, just jot down a keyword every now and then

Tasks	How	Attitude	How
Task-focused moderation	Ensure the research is introduced properly, the questioning line is guarded, answers are evaluated, probes are adequate and the interview is recorded. Do not force things, but respect the respondent's boundaries.	Social-emotional moderation	Ensure there is enough *rapport* by being interested, empathic and inviting[e], be sensitive to the impact the interview may have on the respondent, retain eye contact, be connected and listen actively.

[a] Information on the research project: What is it about, For whom and By whom is it done, What happens to results? has already been given in inviting the respondent to participate. Ensure you do not reveal so much information on the research goal that this could prompt socially acceptable answers but enough information for them to know what is happening.

[b] Confidentiality means that you ensure information provided by the respondent is only known within the research (team). You can do this by keeping transcripts anonymous, keeping transcripts and tapes safe and writing the report in such a manner respondents are not recognizable. Often researchers use fictitious geographical and personal names or only numbers for respondents.

[c] You might want to arrange this when making the appointment for the interview by avoiding cafes and such places as a meeting point. If the interview needs to be conducted in a public place, try to find somewhere with as little background noise as possible, as this strongly affects the quality of your tape.

[d] If the respondent would like to know how you would feel or act in a given situation: 'Do you recognize the feeling that … or Don't you agree?' it is best you let them know that your opinion is not relevant, as you are interested in their opinion. If you sense you would like to answer these types of questions on a person-to-person level, you might want to postpone your answer until after the interview and might indicate this to the respondent.

[e] It is quite difficult to act as if you are interested, inviting and empathic, if you do not feel that way. Although not all research topics are of direct interest to you, you should be aware that if your 'heart' is not in the subject, that will be evident during the interview and will be detrimental to its quality. In such cases, try to tap into your surprise; the willingness to learn more about something if you are confronted with research topics that are not in your sphere of interest directly.

The social-emotional and task-focused conversation guidance should be balanced during the interview, i.e. the interviewer has the same amount of attention for the relationship with the respondent as for the content of the interview.

4.6 PHASES IN AN INDIVIDUAL INTERVIEW

Apart from structuring the interview and the type of questions one can use, different phases can be distinguished in the interview. We have described these briefly in the diagram below. What is not mentioned there is the part played by the surroundings in which the interview takes place which can have quite a large impact on the interview. Our advice, therefore, is to keep this factor under control as best as possible. First, we would like to share a tip that precedes the interview.

In making the appointment for the interview, try to ensure that it takes place in quiet surroundings, preferably where the respondent will not be disturbed and where no others are present[15]. If a respondent needs to be interviewed at his workplace, the researcher might ask whether it is possible to do so in a quiet spot with a minimum of interruption. If the researcher is going to interview someone at home, he might announce that he would prefer to speak to the respondent without family members present. If the interview takes place in public places the interviewer might look for a quiet corner with little background noise.

The following phases can be distinguished in an open individual interview:

---

15. In interviewing certain ethnic groups this can be problematic because of social codes. In such cases, put forward your wishes but accept if they cannot be met. If you cannot interview the respondent on his own, try to steer the interview in such a way that you get responses from the person to be interviewed and that the others are not dominating the conversation. You will probably not always succeed in this.

Diagram 4.1 Phases in the individual interview

> **Opening**
> Make sure the respondent feels at ease. The interview is opened with an introduction on the research aim; a brief outline of the course of the interview and the investigation is given. The interviewer points out that confidentiality is guaranteed. The respondent is asked to authorize the use of recording equipment. If he does, the recording device is switched on.

> **Opening question and probing for depth**
> The opening question is posed, the respondent answers while the interviewer observes him at the same time. Regular eye contact occurs between interviewer and respondent, he probes if necessary and uses other techniques, e.g. humming sounds, silences, repetition, etc., to get *flow* into the interview and to enable depth occurring. If the interviewer has several main questions, he will switch to a next theme at some point.

> **Switching to a new theme with a main question**
> Depending on the type of interview the researcher might have several themes he wants to address. If he feels he has explored a given topic in sufficient depth, he might broach a following theme with a main question. However, he should first check with a summary and open question whether the previous topic has indeed been given thorough attention or if the respondent wishes to add something. In this phase the interviewer will proceed the same way he did in the previous phase: by using related questions, summaries, and other techniques he stimulates the respondent to keep talking and ensures he has both flow and sufficient rapport.

> **Working towards rounding off**
> If the interviewer feels it is time for the interview to come to an end, either because he has obtained sufficient information, the agreed timeframe, or fatigue on the part of the respondent or himself, he might move towards rounding off. He will briefly summarize the main results of the interview in his own words to verify whether everything has been covered and he has understood every point as intended. If subjects are raised that still need to be dealt with, he decides whether this is the right time to do so, or note them for a future interview.

> **Completion**
> The interviewer thanks the respondent for his time and information, switches off the recording equipment and allows some time for a chat afterwards. Sometimes in this final chat the most important information is revealed. If desired and possible, the interviewer makes an appointment for a subsequent interview with a sufficient interval in between for transcription and analysis, thus enabling him to refer to points that were addressed in this interview next time. If it were impossible to schedule a sufficient interval for transcription and analysis, the researcher would better make detailed notes from his keywords and listen to the tape to enable him to have enough material for the following interview.

Tips that apply during the different phases of the interview

- *Opening of the interview*

The interviewer should not seat himself facing the respondent: he might choose a right angle or V-angle, and preferably not with a desk or table in between[16]. For instance, an interview in a sitting area in an office is somewhat more informal and enables a more confidential atmosphere. If the interviewer can influence where the interview takes place, he should do so.

As the above diagram shows, the opening of the interview is quite close to the first question. The opening phrase generally moves into the initial question but it is important that the researcher allows enough time for the opening phase. It is advisable to postpone the starting question until he feels certain the respondent is sufficiently at ease and has no further questions about the research project. Any resistance on the part of the respondent must first be overcome if the interview is to be meaningful. When introducing the project the researcher usually repeats what he has already stated when gaining access to the respondent in writing, verbally or by telephone. Of course, he must have prepared his introduction well, enabling him to give the respondent sufficient information about the purpose of the project without steering his responses in any specific direction by revealing too much information beforehand. If he feels satisfied with the atmosphere and has been given permission to record the interview, he can switch on the recording device and begin. He must have abridged instructions for using the equipment available and practised with it in advance, so he can switch it on easily. He has spare batteries with him as well.

- *Starting question and addressing a new theme*

He is now ready to pose the starting question. We assume that the starting question has already been formulated at the planning stage. What matters now, is to pose the starting question in a way that invites the respondent to answer elaborately. For that purpose he has already created sufficient *rapport* during the introductory phase and has ensured the physical environment is as quiet as possible.

In posing the starting question, not only its formulation and other verbal characteristics, e.g. intonation and wording are important but also the non-verbal messages, e.g. attitude and glance with which it is accompanied. (Gorden, 1998). If a well-formulated question is accompanied by a contradictory non-verbal message, for example of disinterest or impatience, the respondent will not be motivated to answer.

In other words, to get the best possible result the verbal and non-verbal messages must be in harmony. The progress of the interview is determined by the correct use of silences, summaries, probes, follow-up questions, humming, repeating, etc. When passing on to a new theme the interviewer first summarises and allows room for supplementary comment. Only then does he pose the main question for the new theme.

---

16. You may certainly wish to avoid this when interviewing elites or people at their place of work. It is difficult to get them out of their daily role and is a barrier to establishing *rapport*.

- *Working towards finalising*

Concluding an interview is not done abruptly, but gradually. At a given moment the interviewer has gathered sufficient information, time is up, the respondent signals he is ready to stop, or the interviewer loses concentration. He then works towards winding up the interview by pointing this out, and then briefly summarises the main points from the interview to see whether all issues relevant to the respondent have been raised and he has understood everything correctly. If new points arise from this, he has to verify whether the available time and energy levels of both respondent and himself are sufficient for him to proceed. Otherwise he might make a new appointment after switching off the tape recorder.

- *When the interview has ended*

After the tape recorder has been switched off, the interviewer has some time available for a chat as sometimes respondents have a need for this. On the other hand, the interviewer might have promised earlier that he would deal with personal questions after the interview so they can be addressed now. Respondents sometimes reveal the most interesting information once the interview has ended. If this happens in your interview, take your time! If the interview has finally ended, he thanks the respondent for his time and indicates how valuable the interview is for his project. If he generally rewards respondents for their cooperation with a small gift or otherwise, he does so now. Before leaving, he checks whether he has packed all his belongings.

Once the interview has taken place, it is a good idea to review for yourself how things went and what your role in it has been. In Chapter 2 we already discussed at length what you might want to reflect on. Appendix I can guide you in doing so.

4.7   TECHNIQUES AND FLOW IN EQUILIBRIUM

In this chapter we have addressed many practical applications of techniques, aspects of attitude, communication etc. Clearly many things influence the interview situation and the quality of the information gathered. The interviewer has control over some matters, while others are beyond his control. By this time you might have lost courage about ever being able to conduct a good interview. We can reassure you on this point: it is not without reason that in this book we draw so much attention to the flow in an interview. Although an interview is no ordinary conversation, certain aspects of everyday communication are equally valid in an interview. Many things that have run counter to expectations or have been misconstrued by the respondent can be rectified if the interviewer consistently pays close attention and is open to what the respondent says and does. Techniques serve primarily to assist him to purposefully and efficiently obtain the information he would like. Flow is important for the quality of the contact and the information. Skill, which we discussed in Chapter 3, is indispensable to the Art which is the main theme of this chapter. Our motto: prepare yourself well, ensure you are relaxed and have an open mind, and get to work! You will then realise: practice creates perfection. The more interviews you conduct, the more skilful and relaxed you will become. While initially you will mainly rely on Skill, as time passes and your experience grows, you will become increasingly more proficient in the Art.

5 | Designing a focus group

5.1   The origin of focus groups

This chapter will focus on designing group interviews,[1] often named focus groups. The term focus group originated from the work of Robert Merton and Paul Lazersfeld. During the 1940s they did communications research for the U.S military and developed a technique in which respondents were asked to react to a particular scene from a movie or an excerpt from a radio program. This technique was based on a previous content analysis of the stimulus material. It also made use of individual interviews, which Merton and Lazersfeld called *focused interviews* (Merton & Kendall, 2003, Merton, 2003). The group version, which has mainly been used in market research since the 1960s, differs greatly from the original approach by Merton and Lazersfeld. In social sciences, focus groups are used since the eighties of last century.

Generally, a focus group is used as a qualitative method in both fields, sometimes combined with a quantifying method. The methods in both fields vary considerably though; market research is clearly much more time-bound, so the conversation is often tightly structured[2] and data analysis is not emphasized. Social sciences often desire more in-depth information and data is collected and analyzed in a more scientifically oriented manner. The degree of structuring differs considerably, and sometimes the analysis of group interaction is a secondary research purpose (Kitzinger, 2003). Respondents usually are closely involved in the research topic. Morgan thinks this involvement is a primary condition for his 'self-managed groups', in which the conversation is maintained by the group itself.

To compare both fields, the table below summarizes remarks by Morgan (1998) combined with our own experience, to demonstrate the consequences of structuring to a focus group:

---

1. There is no consensus on the precise relationship between focus groups and group interviews. Two views can be distinguished. One group, mostly consisting of social scientists, consider group interviews to be a version of focus groups. In the other view, mostly held by market researchers, focus groups are considered a limited form of group interviews. In this latter view, focus groups have to meet with very strict criteria: they are structured interviews in a homogeneous group of six to ten people, who do not know each other, and meet in a formal environment (Morgan, 2003:324).
2. The conversation guide often shows the number of minutes that is available for each subject.

Table 5.1   Consequences of the degree of structure in a focus group

A more structured approach	A less structured approach
Aim: answer to the research question	Aim: see into the minds of the respondents
Researcher interest dominates	Respondent interest dominates
Questions determine the group discussion	Questions accompany the group discussion
Large amount of specifically formulated questions	Small amount of generally formulated questions
Fixed time available per question	Flexible timing of group discussion
The moderator leads the group discussion	The moderator facilitates the interaction
The moderator steers aberrations back to the research question	The moderator uses aberrations to explore new paths
Respondents talk to the moderator	Respondents talk to each other

From this point onwards, the term focus groups will be used similar to social sciences.

5.2   ADVANTAGES AND DISADVANTAGES OF FOCUS GROUPS

Using a focus group as a data collection strategy has both advantages and disadvantages. Before deciding to use focus groups, these might be considered. As is often the case in research, there is no single solution: the final choice depends on the combination of factors that characterizes a research project. The next table will elaborate on this.

Table 5.2   Advantages and disadvantages of focus groups

Advantages of focus groups	Disadvantages of focus groups
They provide insight into complex behaviour and motivations.	Group composition and the attitude of the moderator are essential for the success or failure of a focus group.
As participants question each other and explain themselves to others, the focus group provides more insight than a collected number of individual interviews would.	Some people are completely overlooked in a focus group. To prevent this, the second, who mainly observes the process and can intervene, is of great importance.
As a result of group dynamics, consensus and disagreement on a theme become more transparent.	Group interaction can result in slightly polarized opinions; alertness of the moderator is in place.
Diversity amongst respondents can be examined during the focus group.	Controlling a group is more complicated than an individual interview. Therefore, fewer topics can be discussed, and the conversation moderator needs much more interview experience.
If respondents share similar backgrounds, an impression of the prevailing values and norms can be obtained. This effect is enhanced if existing social networks are invited into a focus group.	When using existing social networks, certain topics can be taboo.

A more structured approach	A less structured approach
When using existing social networks, people tend to check each other for inconsistencies. This enhances the value of the group interaction as an analytic goal.	People from existing social networks can be hindered in expressing themselves because they are afraid to deviate openly from the prevalent mores.
If people find it hard to give their opinion on certain taboo topics, e.g. because they are a bit shy, a group process can be of assistance to them.	Not all topics are thought suitable for a focus group. Particularly certain taboos or certain undesirable behaviour should not be brought up for discussion in a focus group.[a]
Focus groups are highly suitable for people who are difficult to reach. For example, certain families on the deviant side of the community can be reached this way because they bring each other along.	Hierarchical relationships between respondents in a focus group frustrate the group process. Ensure to avoid this by checking the group composition.
Focus groups can last longer than individual interviews as respondents tire less because they do not always take part in the interaction.	

[a] The literature is divided on this issue: it is often discouraged to discuss taboo topics in focus groups. At the same time researchers who experimented with it, indicated that it worked very well. Again, the researcher should ask what the consequences might be and whether he can deal with those as a moderator. If he thinks the respondents can, he should try it.

5.3   WHAT INFORMATION SHOULD THE FOCUS GROUP PROVIDE?

In designing a focus group[3] one can focus on project-level issues and on so called group-level issues (Morgan, 2003). At **project level**, one consideration is about the type of data the focus group should yield. What would the researcher like to know? It can be useful to standardize the questions to a certain extent for each group to enable comparison of groups. On the other hand, he might decide to take the questions that arise while doing different focus groups, to the next group(s). In this latter case, he starts with a fairly open design. Groups become more structured along the line around a number of issues, based on new insights. An alternative design is Morgan's *funnel* (1998b), in which the researcher works with a fixed set of questions that are used in each focus group and a set of variable questions that are used separately for each focus group. Our experience with this specific approach was positive (Evers, 2001, De Gier et al, 2001). Whatever choice is made, the key question is: what is the main focus of the research: breadth or depth? If one would like to apply some form of generalization (see Smaling 2003), standardization is preferred. If more depth is aimed for, then one of the other approaches is preferable. Another issue at project level is the group composition: should he select homogeneous groups or not? When choosing

---

3. We assume that several focus groups are planned in a research design. If focus groups are used as a stand-alone data collection strategy, this always applies. It is also possible that one uses a single focus group, e.g. experts, to highlight the results from a series of individual interviews from a different viewpoint, but that is not the point we are making here.

homogeneous groups, the need for segmentation is apparent. In that case, groups will be homogeneous on a number of relevant criteria and differ with respect to other criteria. This will be discussed in more detail in section 5.4. The advantage of homogeneous groups is that they facilitate the interaction. The disadvantage is that more groups are needed to get the desired variation. Should the researcher choose for existing groups, e.g. mothers of all children from grade 1a of school X, or not? If interaction patterns or the mores within certain circles are of particular interest, than this would be the best option. Again, the research question will ultimately determine the choice made.

The other dimension, the **group level,** is concerned with how the group is to be moderated. The researcher might choose a standard interview situation with a conversation guide, but he can also choose to use specific elicitation methods. The group can be structured by way of interview techniques and interview model, but also by promoting participation of all respondents. Section 5.7 will elaborate on this. Firstly, it is important to identify which people the researcher would like to approach for his focus groups. The next section will deal with this.

5.4   HOW TO DETERMINE THE SAMPLE FOR YOUR FOCUS GROUPS?

As was briefly discussed in Chapter 2, researchers often select their respondents for a group interview via a purposive sample[4] on the basis of specific background variables. In such a case, the sampling frame of the study can differ considerably. Groups can be composed of people who know or do not know each other, their gender, profession, or the street in which they live. Many criteria can be considered. Therefore, it will be clear that focus group research involves **purposeful sampling**: group composition is carefully determined, based on the objectives of the research and the research question. Besides purposeful selection, **convenience samples**[5] or **self-selected samples**[6] can be used (Morgan, 1998b: 57). The disadvantage of these two methods is that there is no way of controlling how well respondents fit the research topic or to which larger group they belong. Avoiding bias in the selection of respondents is one of the largest pitfalls of non-probability sampling; therefore, convenience sampling and self-selection mostly are left out in advance.

---

4. Purposive sampling is one of the 'non-probability sampling' methods (Russel Bernard, 2006: 147). These methods are the counterpart for the probabilistic sampling methods, based on probability reasoning. Other non-probability samples (Boeije, 't Hart & Hox 2009: 227) are: a snowball sample, a convenience sample and a self-selected sample.
5. Anyone who would like to participate is accepted. So anyone available for the focus group will participate in it.
6. People enrol themselves as respondent. The so-called 'professional respondents', who participate so often in research that they cannot actually be regarded the average citizen the researcher is seeking, is a real danger of this sampling format.

When thinking about group composition, some rules of thumb are available:
- The ease with which respondents will exchange their views concerning the research topic. This point determines the exact composition of each group separately; respondents have to 'match' a little. In research we did in Curaçao (Evers, 2001), for example, a group was composed of both policy makers and implementation staff members of various organizations, who worked in the same policy area, e.g. youth.
- The aim one has with the focus groups. Both the composition of all groups together and the composition of each group separately are important, because this determines the type of data to expect. In the same study in Curaçao, all (non-)governmental organizations within eight institutional spheres were mapped first and a selection of these organizations was entered into the purposive sample. They were then asked to delegate an employee to participate in a focus group which was organized around certain organizations in one policy area.

Group composition
The way respondents fit in a group cannot always be determined in advance. Especially when conflicting views exist, this fit can fall short. However, it might be better to avoid inviting persons with conflicting interests into one group, as well as persons who are in hierarchical relationships with each other. If the researcher is doubtful about group matches, it is better to start with large mixed groups. If this results in identifying people that do not fit within a certain group, or certain subcategories of respondents are discovered, then groups can be composed later on, using those selection criteria.

The main **demographic characteristics** used in selecting group members are:
- Gender;
- Race or ethnicity;
- Age
- Town / district / neighbourhood / street;
- Education;
- Occupation;
- Income;
- Marital or family status.

Although **homogeneity** encourages positive group dynamics, the degree to which members agree on the research subject is more important for group dynamics than their demographic similarities. For example, in a research project concerning bereavement all group members are widowed but they come from very different backgrounds. Those backgrounds are less relevant because they share a common experience, i.e. losing one's partner. In market research it is discouraged to put men and women in a group together because of their differing views on products. In social science research this is often less relevant. The point is how the group responds to the objectives of the research project and the research question and whether gender differences are to be expected. Whether to use **existing groups** or not primarily depends on the research question. In a group of people who know each other, many things are not discussed because group members are familiar with each other's opinion about them. On the one hand, this is an advantage because it saves time but it can certainly be detrimental if the researcher is looking for just that implicit knowledge or mores. In the latter case a group of people who do not know each other will be chosen.

Group segmentation
To enable group-member comparison or between-groups comparison, **segmentation** is applied. In using segmentation as a sampling strategy, the researcher considers in advance on what aspects of their research question people might respond differently. Next, he decides whether that difference is interesting enough to justify including a separate segment of people who meet that criterion. Segmentation often means determining whether the potential respondents meet certain criteria. Sometimes the researcher might have to do a small telephone survey first to trace possible respondents. Conclusively, in deciding whether or not segmentation is an adequate sampling strategy, the next questions can be considered:
- Considering the research question, which categories of respondents should be included?
- What possible differences and similarities might be relevant with regard to the research topic?
- Who would feel left out if they were not invited to participate?
- Are possible differences between groups of respondents interesting enough for the research question to justify putting together several types of groups?

It is not only possible to segment on the bases of the aforementioned demographic characteristics, but also based on **other criteria** that seem relevant to the research question, e.g.:
- Users versus non-users. Note: non-users are often difficult to recruit and sometimes have little to report. This makes them a difficult target group;
- People with a certain experience and those who still have to go through that experience, e.g. giving birth;
- People with certain social roles or with certain positions within organizations;
- People who have a certain vision, belief or religion. Note: this might be dangerous because people who share a vision or opinion might have nothing else in common. This might disrupt the group dynamics. If the research is mainly focused on a shared vision and belief, then presumably this will compensate the difference between respondents in other areas.

Suppose a certain segment is the most important but some other distinct segments exist which are less important. The researcher could then choose to organize multiple groups within this core segment, alongside a single group for each of the other less relevant segments. This enables him to get sufficiently detailed data from the core segment, while at the same time collecting some data for comparison (Morgan, 1998b: 66).

5.5 ORGANIZATION OF FOCUS GROUPS

Planning and conducting focus groups is more time consuming than individual interviews. It is advised to make a timeline for the project from start to finish, i.e. the reporting phase. In focus groups this is even more important, since their organization can be quite difficult and takes some effort. In planning the project, the researcher should keep holidays in mind, including those of particular religions or ethnicities if they apply to the target population.

In order to get a grip on the organization of focus groups, the researcher might ask himself the following questions in advance:
• Is secretarial or administrative support available for the organization of focus groups? Someone must organize it all, keep track of who will come and who has cancelled, remind people about the meeting or call them if they are not showing up on time, etc.
• Is a moderator available within the research team or should external expertise be hired?
• Is a second needed for the moderator or not? If so, is someone available to act as a second during the focus groups? Which arrangements will be made between moderator and their second about their respective roles in the focus group?
• How will the focus group be recorded: minute taking, recording keywords, audio or visual recording, or both? What is the role of the second in this? What equipment is needed? Is that equipment available, should it be rented, or maybe bought?
• Who will work on the notes of the focus group, or transcribe the recording? Is that expertise present, or should it be hired and at what price? When can transcription start and how much time will be needed per focus group?
• Who will design the conversation guide or the questions for the focus group?
• Are other elicitation techniques desirable? Who will provide their content and take care of logistics?
• What role does the commissioner of the research play in the design, execution, and report of the focus groups? In market research, this role is often prominent. In applied research it is advisable to consider this beforehand (Evers, 2003).

- Where will the focus groups be held? Will they be spread across the country, or will respondents be invited to a central location? To put it differently, will the researcher travel to respondents or will he let them come to his location? Is the location available and affordable?
- Who takes care of catering during the focus groups?
- Is it necessary to transport respondents to the location or to give an allowance for travel expenses? Do respondents receive a small gift for participating and if so, who will take care of that?
- What moments will be suitable for the target group to organize focus groups: during the day or evening, or during weekends?

All these questions are relevant when preparing the project.

While preparing and planning, the researcher must decide which follow-up activities will take place to ensure the participation of respondents. For instance, a confirmation letter with directions, a reminder telephone call just before the meeting, etc. These are included in his planning scheme.

He might ensure the recording equipment has a microphone capable of handling a group. This certainly requires a higher quality microphone and sometimes even a separate omnidirectional microphone will be needed.

Arrangements will be made with transcribers on how to deal with the audio files and how to return the transcript and audio files to the research team in such a way that confidentiality is guaranteed.

The right location will be selected and confirmed it is available at the desired moments. It is advantageous to choose a location near a public transport facility which is also accessible to wheelchairs.

5.6   ELICITATION TECHNIQUES FOR FOCUS GROUPS

In Chapter 3 some elicitation techniques were discussed which can be applied to both individual and group interviews. Besides these, several other group techniques exist which make use of the presence of more respondents. Group techniques not only enable the researcher to see how people react to what others suggest, but they also provide more in-depth knowledge about the differences or the similarities mentioned. Sometimes the intention is to reach consensus. e.g. the Metaplan method might seek priorities or ranking preferences but this is not always necessary. For instance, the **diversity** which occurs is in all its depth the object of the focus group. Focus groups often achieve less depth on an individual respondent level but bring better understanding on the width or variety of the subject and explore that in-depth. The researcher could even consider organizing several sessions with the same group of respondents to gain in-depth understanding at the individual level as well. The only thing that would prevent this is the possible restrictive effect of the group process which could make people more hesitant to provide sensitive information in comparison to a one-on-one situation. On the other hand, focus groups are known to encourage people to sometimes cross the line and provide certain information because of the recognition within the group.

In the table below, a number of group techniques from market research and applied social science research will be discussed.

Table 5.3   Elicitation techniques for focus groups

Technique	Method	Examples
Personification	Originated in market research. It asks respondents to describe a product in terms of people. The intention is to elicit implicit associations with the product first and then use the group interview to gain in-depth understanding.	Cf. Van Fessem in Evers, 2007.
Brainstorm or Ping-Pong in pairs	Respondents in groups or in pairs are asked to rapidly name free associations concerning a question or task from the researcher. These associations are noted and explored in a group interview or through other methods.	Instruction can be found in Bikker and Temme (1999). The method was used in conjunction with metaplan in De Gier a.o. (2001).
Metaplan	The contributed information of the respondents is organized and categorized, possibly along dimensions designed by the researcher.	Instruction can be found in Bikker and Temme (1999). The method was used in association with ping-pong brainstorming in De Gier a.o. (2001).
Inversion	In inversion, respondents are asked to brainstorm about the opposite situation of the research problem. Suggested strategies are then reversed again to the problem, as sometimes the solution can be found in the inversion.	For example, if the problem is how to improve the quality of care, nurses would be asked to brainstorm about ways to deteriorate care.
Complaints and Jubilations	Respondents are invited to write down any complaints regarding the research topic on the complaint wall and to write all positive aspects on the jubilation wall. By being confronted with other people's points, this creates new items. The points are listed as starting points for the group interview.	A description can be found in Bikker and Temme (1999) or Hampsink and Hagedoorn (2006).
Nominal group technique	Respondents are asked to discuss opinions on the current topic, based on their individual ideas. They then select and rank a number of opinions that they think are most relevant.	This technique is mainly used if hierarchical positions may affect data collection or if one would like to transcend established ways of thinking in an organization. Cf. De Ruyter & Scholl (2001) and Vogel & Verhallen (1983).

Technique	Method	Examples
Q-sort	Based on literature or other sources a collection of propositions is designed. Respondents are asked to prioritize these according to their own preference and explain their prioritization. Using a type of factor analysis, a statistical variable reduction technique, the preference profile for each respondent is determined. Next, this profile is aggregated to the sample.	Combination of qualitative and quantifying techniques were used in a study into care preferences of adolescents with chronic diseases (Jedeloo a.o., 2006).

There are many more group techniques available than those listed here (Van Fessem in Evers, 2007, Stalpers 2007, Hampsink & Hagedoorn 2006). By naming some we hope to inspire you to experiment with these methods. Dare to deviate from the track every now and then.

5.7   STRUCTURING THE FOCUS GROUP

This section will return briefly to the ways of structuring that can be utilized during the focus group. In Chapter 3 the opening-the-locks-model, the river model and the tree-and-branches model were discussed, including the dominant question types used in each model. We will discuss those with regard to a focus group here. Morgan's funnel model will be discussed as a specific focus group model. Next, we will examine the roles the researcher can take as a moderator.

5.7.1   *Interview models and types*

As discussed in Chapter 3, the researcher can choose between specific interview models, e.g. the **opening-the-locks model**, the **river model**, and the **tree-and-branches model** and determine whether they are particularly interested in a **thematic** or a **cultural interview**. In addition to these models with an increasing level of structuring by the researcher, Morgan (1998b: 49) distinguishes the additional **funnel model**. In comparison with the models discussed earlier, the funnel model can be regarded as a combination of the opening-the-locks model and the tree-and-branches model. The researcher designs one or two very broad open questions, the upperfunnel with which he starts the focus group to enable free association. Furthermore, the researcher notes four key themes on the conversation guide which he definitely would like to address as well. This is called the middle of the funnel. The focus group's session is concluded with a discussion about tightly defined aspects of the themes that were raised[7] which is the bottom funnel.

---

7. It is unclear whether Morgan refers to probes based on topics which were dealt with earlier or the testing of hypotheses or assumptions about the research topic that the researcher made beforehand.

Although focus groups are often seen and used as a more structured form of interviewing which is organized thematically, this need not be the case. There is no reason not to choose for a more open interview model, as this may very well provide endowed information. The researcher should be aware, however, that the more open the interview, the more interview experience he needs as a moderator.

5.7.2 Moderator roles and styles

Chapter 3 discussed the different roles a moderator can utilize. Some of these correspond to the roles in an individual interview but they have a slightly different approach in a group and are often more complex because of the group dynamics.[8] In addition, a number of roles are specifically intended for a focus group.

Host: In a focus group respondents usually go to a location which the researcher specifies, as opposed to an individual interview in which the respondent is mostly approached in their own environment. Therefore, in a group interview the researcher clearly has a role as a host, next to his research role. People should be made to feel at ease and that they are comfortable. This refers to the room temperature, noise control, and the availability of food and drink.

Director: The researcher is responsible for the proper course of the interview and a careful introduction and explanation of the focus group rules. Explaining the research purpose and what will happen with the results is part of this introduction. Another aspect of this role is ensuring everyone gets sufficient room to talk, and preventing dominating personalities' talking over more timid respondents. This role can sometimes require many navigating skills.

8. Be careful not fall into the trap of being a serial interviewer during your group interview. Although you need to ensure that everyone is heard, it is better for the data quality if they take turns spontaneously. Try to encourage the group members to respond to each other.

Timekeeper: In focus groups, time issues are usually is more urgent than in individual interviews. In market research this is even stronger than in social science research. The researcher needs to monitor time and control digression. This requires navigating skills.

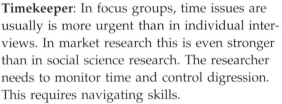

Manager: there are always people in a group who communicate through subtle nonverbal signals, such as a particular eye rolling or seeking eye contact with the moderator. Therefore, it is important to continually 'scan' the group for these signals and act on them, sometimes at a later stage. It is helpful to have a second available, who is explicitly instructed to observe the group process, enabling the moderator to concentrate on the content of the interview. The two of them can agree whether the second is free, in an appropriate time, to intervene on these types of signals. This role requires teamwork.

Summarizer: In focus groups the role of summarizer is even more comprehensive than in individual interviews. Summarizing in focus groups is not only used to ensure the researcher understood what was said, but it is also used to get to the core of the whole discussion. This requires much concentration and abstraction.

Challenger/schemer: Especially in a focus group it can sometimes be useful to slightly stir up a conversation in order to gain information on underlying values, or to get to contradictions. This requires careful wording[9], good timing and sensing the atmosphere well.

---

9. Especially in these situations it is important to be able to articulate a neutral and an open question in which no opinion can be heard. People tend to suspect you have more sympathy for the other group; this exerts pressure on your position. Be sure to place yourself outside the opposition you are looking for when using this type of intervention.

Investigator: The researcher has a specific research goal and a research question which form the framework for the interview. Professionalism is required.

Linesman: This role supplements that of the researcher: not only knowing exactly what he is looking for but also being responsible for monitoring its boundaries. On the one hand, this means not cutting a possible interesting sideline too fast, as he does not know what relevant information he might exclude. On the other hand, it means reflecting constantly on whether information is still within the big picture. This role requires a considerable amount of concentration.

Atmosphere Maker: The interviewer ensures that a safe atmosphere is created where people are willing and daring to show vulnerable aspects about themselves. It requires much sensitivity and sometimes flexibility to respond to issues.

Team player: The division of roles between the moderator and the second is done beforehand. In general, the moderator is responsible for the content of the interview, while the second observes the interaction and manages the recording device. They can agree on certain signals to be used to inform each other about matters that evolve during the interview. The second does not intervene substantially in the interview, unless it appears that the moderator is 'missing' a respondent in their questioning. In such a case he signals the moderator that this respondent would like to bring an idea forward. In our experience, this works smoothly. We are in the habit of checking with each other after each focus group if the partnership actually went smoothly or if additional arrangements are needed.

Teacher: Sometimes the interviewer needs to explain matters to respondents, e.g. the objective of the study or some abstract notions about which he would like to collect information. This requires a thorough preparation and the researcher will have to familiarize himself with the research population to devise the explanation in a comprehensible manner. This role requires empathy.

Seeker/searcher: The interviewer is looking for the experiences or knowledge of the respondents and assumes that he is on track if he asks the right questions. Technical interview skills are required.

Auto-monitor: The interviewer is constantly aware of himself and monitors whether he is properly conducting the interview; a role that requires much practice and self-reflection.

Detective: This role is additional to the seeker/searcher because people do not reveal everything, even though they are asked the right questions. Much sensitivity to nonverbal signals and the atmosphere is required to find what they are – possibly – suppressing. This role requires unconditional presence of all the senses.

In addition to these desirable and sometimes necessary roles are the undesirable ones:

Commissioner: Respondents sometimes see the interviewer as a representative of the person or organization who commissioned the research. It is important to properly explain the relationship, as well as what will happen with the results which may or may not be anonymized. Especially in commercial (market) research, the commissioner is often involved in data collection; either by watching the focus group behind a glass mirror or participating in the focus group. In such a case, clear appointments on roles and responsibilities are even more important and these should be communicated to respondents.

Social worker: A situation can arise in an interview where respondents implicitly or explicitly ask for help which might range from the odd job to something which resembles a dependency relationship. Where to draw the line is sometimes difficult to identify in advance. The researcher should not put himself in the position of a 'saviour' or counsellor, as he is neither. It might be better to point the respondent towards professional help.

Messenger: Sometimes respondents or commissioners would like to use the researcher as their messenger, either to protect their interests or to convey a painful message (Evers, 2003). Although qualitative research is aimed at giving respondents a 'voice' and make their voices heard, the researcher is not a messenger. It is up to the researcher to achieve valid results from the mix of voices which often resemble different interests.

Companion: Respondents often ask the researcher for confirmation while he at the same time identifies with their story to a different extent. His role, however, is not that of a companion, but of a researcher. Empathy can also be present without statements regarding one self. If you feel these are needed, preferably keep them for after the interview.

5.8   PLANNING YOUR PROJECT

In sections 2.10 and 3.9 we extensively discussed planning to obtain access to the population and planning individual interviews in relation to transcription. This section, therefore, will be limited to the planning aspects which are specific to focus groups. As was indicated earlier, the **logistics** of focus groups are quite time consuming so should be taken into account while planning the research.

It is advised to allocate sufficient time for the **recruitment of respondents**. Not only finding respondents takes time but organising respondents to be available at the same time for the focus group is yet another challenge. Depending on the target population, this might be tricky. In our experience, for instance, a letter can hardly recruit Moroccan women, while scientists are hard to recruit all together. In short, allocate enough time and if possible, recruit people by telephone or in person instead of in writing, by e-mail or via the Internet. For some hard to reach groups, it is recommended to announce in writing that you will telephone or approach them in person about their participation. The method of contacting respondents excludes certain respondents, so the researcher will ensure they have sufficient substitute candidates per focus group.

As the interviewer hosts the focus groups, he has to arrange the location, the catering and the tidying up afterwards. Is it needed to purchase goods, wash them or return something? Is the site inspected beforehand on the presence of the necessary resources for the focus group, i.e. flipchart, whiteboard, etc.?

It is important in focus group research to plan enough time between groups to enable transcription and possible interim analysis. How many focus groups are planned depends on the structure of the sample: the amount of segmentation pursued is a function of the total number of groups needed. Of course, this partly depends on the homogeneity of the target population. A number of six to twelve groups is common in a relatively homogeneous population or in an applied research project. Within PhD research or in a heterogeneous population, the researcher needs to put more groups together.

A focus group, as was mentioned before, is very intense for the moderator, often much more so than for the respondents. It usually takes between three and four hours in the social sciences. This restricts the number of groups that can be done per day to one. After all, the moderator needs time to process the information afterwards in order to have an open mind for the next group. Within market research this is different; because of the tight structuring and focus on costs (Van Fessem in Evers, 2007) focus groups take much less time and several are done per day. It is advisable to allocate some time for the debriefing of the group with the second afterwards. In market research, this time is often used for a preliminary analysis of the results.

Aspects that put a burden on the allocation of time are the relative inexperience of the researcher or the team in conducting focus group research, the lack of a directory from which respondents can be drawn,[10] the organization of the focus groups at various locations around the country and detailed data-storage and analysis. Whatever the researcher chooses, he needs to ensure the proper organization of logistics surrounding the project, as well as the allocation of time and registration of matters.

5.9   CONCLUSION: SIMILARITIES AND DIFFERENCES BETWEEN INDIVIDUAL
           INTERVIEWS AND FOCUS GROUPS

It is obvious that designing a focus group encompasses some similarities to an individual interview. These are mainly found in the interview type, its model and the matching conversation guide, as well as in some roles the moderator can utilize.
There are also major differences between the two interview approaches. These are mainly found in the logistics process, which takes much more time, effort and man-hours in focus groups. Designing a good sample is quite a challenge and the recruitment of respondents is more time consuming. Moreover, the interviewer needs to think carefully about the number of issues he would like to address in the focus group and whether to pursue comparison by using a rather strict conversation guide for all groups or to continuously adapt the conversation guide between groups.
The comparative assessment between focus groups and individual interviews is not an easy one. Of course, the research question and the target population play a role in this choice, but we believe the interview experience is a criterion that should be considered as well. In addition, the researcher may consider doing both: individual interviews to gain deeper understanding following a focus group, or as a preparation for a focus group. Chapter 6 will examine the practice of conducting focus groups.

---

10. Especially in market research people are used to working with agencies that maintain directories of potential respondents. In social science research this is less often the case, unless you approach people via some institutional channel.

6 | Conducting a focus group

Chapter 4 described conducting an individual interview in practical terms. Some aspects that apply to focus groups are discussed here as well such as question types, interview models, patterns of interaction during the interview and points of particular interest for an interview. In order to avoid repetition, you also might read sections 4.1 to 4.5, even if you only plan to do focus groups. In this chapter only matters that are specific to focus groups are discussed.

6.1 THE ORGANIZATIONAL ASPECTS OF FOCUS GROUP RESEARCH

In Chapter 5 aspects which need to be taken into consideration in designing the sample and organizing the focus groups were discussed at length. Depending on the research topic the group size will also vary[1] between six and ten people. To determine the actual size of the group, it is useful to have a look at how much time each respondent would have for his own experience or opinion and whether it would be sufficient. This of course also depends on the number of questions that must be answered, the time that has been allocated, and the possible verbosity of the respondent. The following table gives an estimation of a certain number of questions in a period of time and what that means per respondent in the group. You might want to try your questions with some friends or colleagues and clock the time they need to answer them.

---

1. If the research topic is emotionally charged, you will need to allocate more time for the story in general because of the emotions attached.

Table 6.1 Relating the number of respondents, questions and available time

Number of respondents	Number of questions[a]	Time – in minutes – allocated to the group	Minutes available per person per question
6	6	240	6.5
6	6	120	3.2
8	5	240	6
8	5	120	3
10	4	240	6
10	4	120	3

[a] The reference is to the main question and probes, or topics that the researcher would like to address in the focus group.

This diagram shows the amount of time each respondent has at his disposal theoretically. Of course, not every respondent has the need to tell his whole story because people often have similar experiences and join in on the stories of others. A good rule of thumb is: the deeper the subject of study, the more time each respondent needs for his story. Adjust the number of questions accordingly.

In the box below, we ordered the main points to consider in making a group composition.

Tips for a careful group composition

When using focus groups, putting together a purposeful sample and composing the right groups within that sample is very important for data quality and the generalization level which can be achieved (Morgan, 1998b; Remmers & Greenland, 2006).

Factors in compiling the sample are:
• Demographic characteristics of respondents;
• Generalization level the researcher aims for which determines how much use is made of segmentation in the group composition;
• The research goal; is it knowledge-oriented, practical, or action-oriented? This affects whether or not the researcher would like the people in the group to know each other or not.

In compiling the individual groups, some other factors might play a role:
• To what extent does the researcher expect people to communicate with each other about the subject? Group members have to 'fit'.
• Are any conflicts of interest expected among respondents? If so, it is better not to put those persons in a group.
• Is there a functional hierarchy present between participants? If so, it is better to avoid placing them in the same group.

- With regard to the research objective: are homogeneous groups preferable or should they be heterogeneous? Are existing groups to be preferred or not?
- Which segmentation criteria are to be combined in a group?
- What impact or emotional charge might the research topic have on respondents?

If respondents are selected and recruited and the focus group can take place, a few *practical issues* need to be dealt with. We identify them below.

- To prevent creating a 'meeting' kind of atmosphere in which the researcher personifies the chairman, preferably use a round or oval table.
- Use mugs instead of cups and saucers and combine them with wooden or plastic stirrers to avoid a high noise level on the audio file, which makes it hard to transcribe.
- If the recording device does not come with a very good microphone that can be used in a group – this needs to be tried beforehand, e.g. during a meeting or during a meal at home – consider buying an omnidirectional microphone and place it in the middle of the table. The recording device must have a separate microphone input[2] available. Remember to have spare batteries for the recording device and possibly also a separate microphone.
- Ensure nameplates are available for the participants to write their names on at both sides, so the people next to them are able to read it. It is best to have 1.5-3 mm markers available as well.
- Set up a flipchart with markers to make notes and discuss them with the group or if fictitious names are used for participants to share sensitive information in a depersonalized manner.
- Post-it notes of different sizes and colours may be convenient to use in certain elicitation techniques and ensure sufficient pens or pencils are available for participants to work with.

6.2   THE USE OF DIFFERENT QUESTION TYPES AND INTERVIEW MODELS

We have discussed different **question types**, i.e. main questions, probes, and follow-up questions in section 4.2. Naturally, the question types used are adapted to the type of interview. In this section, we briefly mention which are dominant in the various models.

In the **opening-the-locks model**, probes are used most often to follow the respondent in his line of thought, as long as it fits within the boundaries of the research topic. Even if this does not seem to be the case, the researcher will let the respondent elaborate at first, just to see if no unexpected association of ideas rises

---

2. For devices with a built-in microphone this is often not the case, so this is a point to consider when buying one.

which might be very interesting in relation to the research topic. The researcher can involve the other respondents in this probe by asking how they experience the subject. This model will, however, be more difficult to handle in groups; it is likely the researcher will opt for the river model.

When using the **river model**, there is usually only one main question which will be explored in full into several adjacent streams by using follow-up questions. The researcher structures the current discussion by ensuring that any follow-up question and matching probes are kept within the surfacing theme as to prevent being drowned in secondary issues. This is more relevant in a group because of the many 'voices' that may go astray. Therefore, we strongly recommend having a second present.

In the tree-and-branches model, the research topic is considered as a whole in whose context sub-themes are dealt with. Therefore, the time spent on probing sub-themes is quite limited and the researcher mainly relies on the predesigned main questions and probes. In this model, the researcher can very well invite group members to respond. In the **funnel model**, main questions and probes dominate as well.

6.3   INTERACTION PATTERNS DURING A FOCUS GROUP

Different patterns of interaction during an interview, which were discussed in Chapter 4, also apply to a focus group. Therefore, in the next paragraphs we will only discuss those interaction patterns which are typical of focus groups. The general interaction patterns that apply can be found in section 4.3.

6.3.1   *Moderator and respondent behaviour*

The **group interaction** is emphatically taken into consideration. For example, notorious 'complainants' can drag the entire group along if the researcher does not intervene. The same applies to dominant personalities[3] and experts or people who like to present themselves as one. In intervening, the researcher often lets the person know he respects his point of view, yet he stresses that other views are possible and welcome and to him are of equal importance. The researcher might make his neutrality explicit in such cases. If dominant personalities and experts participate in the group it might be advisable to explicitly invite others to

---

3. Krueger (1998:58) suggests placing dominant persons in the group next to the conversation leader. This dominant behaviour often already manifests itself upon entering the room and in the small talk that precedes the actual interview. This will enable the moderator to control their input by way of . If this placement or the non-verbal clues do not work, the researcher might verbally invite other group members to express their views.

express their views on the topic. Certainly the more timid personalities in the group may be reluctant to speak as a result of the dominant behaviour of others.

In **moderating** the group, the researcher can use non-verbal signals, e.g. position his hands low in a 'stop' signal if he would like to indicate that someone must finalise, break eye contact when someone continues on an irrelevant topic too long. He can use verbal signals as well: interruption when people are talking together, explain rules for the group communication at the beginning, i.e. everyone is equally important, let others finish, he can act when someone is too dominant by emphatically letting others express their opinions. The researcher can also exercise control over the seats of respondents, e.g. if people are constantly whispering among each other, he can ask the group during the break to take a different place at the table. Finally, he can request people who clearly disturb the group and are unable to adapt their behaviour, to leave. Until now, we have not yet experienced a situation where we had to apply such stringent measures.

6.3.2   *Behaviour of respondents*

Working with **existing groups** can demand extra requirements from the moderator. People can show a united front that always agrees with one another, or can boycott the group. They can talk amongst each other or expose revealing looks and sounds, such that the others feel excluded. In an existing group, many matters remain unspoken because they know each other's viewpoint. On the one hand, this can be an advantage because it saves time, but it can certainly be detrimental if you are looking for just those implicit habits or behaviour which seem obvious.

Another aspect to consider when dealing with group interviews is dealing with statements by respondents addressed to others, e.g. personal attacks, comments on what the other said in a personal sense or an exchange of irrelevant information. **Clarification of the rules** at the beginning of the group interview, particularly if one does not agree with the views of others to still respect them and not to be personal in their remarks towards others, is essential to prevent these problems within a group. This enables the researcher to refer to these rules and mention that everyone agreed to them in the beginning. Of course, the researcher should ensure they do so at the start of the group.

An **ethical dilemma** arises for the researcher if participants give advice to others during the group interview which to him is known to be false. The question is how to deal with this because it interferes with his neutral interview role. He might choose to let it pass by if the advice is harmless. If, on the other hand, the advice is harmful, he could possibly refer back to it at the end of the interview.

6.3.3   *Behaviour of the conversation leader and the second*

As was mentioned before, it is very convenient to **work in pairs** during group in-terviews and distribute tasks. The second might focus on the recording device and interaction and non-verbal signals especially while the researcher concen-trates on the content of the information and its relation to the problem statement. In short, the interviewer as moderator is responsible for listening actively and all associated interview interventions and the second mainly focuses on observing. In addition, the second can intervene in the interview process if appropriate, based on his observations. Discussing each focus group afterwards to monitor the cooperation and – if necessary – adjust the agreements, has been useful to us.

6.4   STRUCTURING THE FOCUS GROUP

The **interview model** and its matching conversation guide combined with the **moderating style** will determine the structuring of the focus group. Additionally, one might say that the degree of structuring also indicates whose perspective is dominant. In a structured group, the perspective of the research team is domi-nant; in a less structured group the perspective of the respondents dominates. Within social sciences, the ideal situation would often be that the group itself works towards the topics without too much control of the moderator. Our ex-perience shows that this often will succeed with a well-prepared and thoughtful design. The researcher has determined all the possible topics related to the re-search subject beforehand and incorporated these in the conversation guide. In the group session itself, the respondents will mention most of the themes sponta-neously but often in a different order from the conversation guide. This is not a problem if the interviewer is the one that had designed the conversation guide and as such is able to follow the group and improvise. Even with a rather long and detailed conversation guide the interview style can still be to follow the re-spondents. In our experience, working on the design himself will make the re-searcher a better moderator; because of this he is quite familiar with the whole research topic and all of its subtopics. This certainly has a positive influence and might even be essential for the quality of the interview and the possibilities there are to respond to events happening. Within social sciences, a focus group is still largely characterized as an open interview that takes place within a group forma-tion. In this context, it is highly relevant that the interviewer can respond to what is happening and use proper probes. The table below provides an overview of the different interview styles and matching moderator styles.

Table 6.2   Number of questions per interview model and matching moderator style

Degree of structuring	Questions	Conversation leading style
Less structured (Opening-the-locks model)	Just one or two broadly formulated main questions are designed, which invite exploration	The moderator allows the group to choose their own path and stimulates respondents to express their own feelings about the subject, their thoughts regarding it, and their experiences with the subject.
Half structured (Funnel model)	Firstly, one or two broadly formulated main questions are designed that explore the research topic. Next, three to four key issues, related to the research topic should be addressed. These themes are predefined by the researcher and considered important. Often they surface spontaneously, initiated by the starting question. The conversation concludes with a discussion on well-defined aspects from within the predefined themes. This might happen spontaneously as well, based on the foregoing.	The moderating role varies at the different stages of the funnel. In the beginning he allows exploration, in the second stage he guides gently towards the predefined themes. In the final stage he purposefully probes about aspects of the themes that he thinks were insufficiently treated in the previous stages.
Half structured (River model)	In this model the moderator starts with one or two main questions and explores emerging themes by asking follow-up questions and probes.	The moderator explores a theme until he is satisfied that everything has been said about it. He then continues with a follow-up question on a different theme which was brought up by respondents earlier on. Again, this theme will be further explored until he is satisfied, and so on.
More structured (Tree-and-branches model)	In this model the moderator uses a larger number of clearly defined questions. The questions deal with specific research goals and should, therefore, be precise and clear. Note: too many questions often signal that the study design was insufficient or that the researcher is using a very deductive approach which is more suitable for a survey.	The moderator controls group dynamics while aiming to keep the group focused on the subject. In this model the moderator obviously is more in control.

6.5   POINTS OF PARTICULAR INTEREST IN MODERATING A FOCUS GROUP

The points of particular interest in conducting an individual interview, mentioned in Chapter 4, also apply to a group interview. As it is a group of people that needs to be moderated in a focus group, some additional matters apply as well. We will discuss these below.

It is important to ensure at the beginning of the focus group that people are at ease quickly and that they get a chance to talk soon. The **introduction** can be used for this. People can be invited, on the basis of a brief instruction with the type of information the moderator would like them to share, to introduce themselves and to associate their names with their voices on the tape, which is needed for the person transcribing. If some differences in background characteristics within the group are expected which might lead to friction, it is wise not to mention this in the instruction. For example: if the group focuses on the experiences with a particular public institution, the education level of some participants might be intimidating to others. If the level of education is relevant to the research question the sample is segmented on this aspect. For the conversation though, this is not important. The researcher then ensures to design his instruction in such a way that participants do not mention this during the introduction.

In explaining the **rules of conversation**, the phasing of which will be discussed in the next section, everyone is asked to switch their **mobile telephones off**. Of course, this applies to the moderator and the second as well. Participants are asked at the beginning of the first interview to **mention their names** before they make their point. If they forget, the moderator might mention their name in his response, to facilitate transcription later on.

Participants are invited to help themselves to **drinks and snacks** at any moment. This gives them the opportunity to be otherwise engaged during the interview as well. It is advisable to have water available besides coffee, tea and soft drinks. It is best to display these at the centre of the table or on a side table but it will cause much noise on the recording device if people are shifting their seats constantly to get up for a drink or a snack.

The moderator, should plan for a **washroom or smoke break** about every hour. He might announce this at the beginning of the focus group, so people know that the break is coming. If possible, he might do this at times when an issue in his opinion is completed and before the next issue is raised. If a topic lasts too long and the hour has already passed, then the moderator could suggest the group to postpone the break until the current issue is completed. It is best to let matters run their course, pick up signals from the group, and let the group dynamics guide the process.

Emotional utterances or **highly personal statements** can sometimes have a considerable impact on the group interview. Such situations are to be expected with certain research topics. As a moderator, it is advisable to be prepared for such a case in advance by thinking about possible ways of dealing with them. In emotionally charged issues, the moderator would like to prevent the focus group from becoming a support group, so he adjusts his questions accordingly. In morally charged issues, people may tell something about themselves which is morally reprehensible to others. Again, the moderator can customize the questions to make the interview more impersonal and ask participants to leave aside whether their answers are about themselves or reflect behaviour they have observed or heard from others.[4] Krueger (1998:64) suggests writing a number of girls' names and boys' names on a flipchart which can be used to anonymize such a story.

The main advantage of a focus group is both the **diversity of opinions and experiences** which can be collected while at the same time getting in-depth information about them. To ensure this, the moderator has to work consciously on triggering the diversity of opinions, the pitfall being to proceed as a 'serial interviewer' (Krueger, 1998:48). In the latter case, he appeals to the respondents one by one. Spontaneous group exchange would be the goal to strive for. This might happen if the moderator decides on his outline and monitors this by the timely deployment of probes and follow-up questions. As spontaneous group interactions are very informative, he should make use of it whenever possible. The **'self-managed group'** (Morgan 1988, 2003) is an extreme form in which the moderator completely refrains from any direction and sits outside the group.

While the senses and concentration in an individual interview are primarily focused on moving along and actively listening to one person, in a focus group this has to be done with several people concurrently. For such an interview, **much experience** is needed and in general it is more **exhaustive** to the moderator than an individual interview. However, for the participants, a focus group is less tiring than an individual interview because they are not constantly involved actively. This means that a focus group can take longer than an individual interview; we have had group interviews lasting four hours. In order to see this through it is important for the moderator to be well equipped physically and mentally, as well as being prepared with a proper conversation guide.

If any elicitation techniques are used in combination with a flipchart or whiteboard for taking notes, e.g. the complaints and jubilations wall, one might consider to have one or more video cameras with a wide-angle lens available to record the interaction in addition to the normal **audio recording**. If the interaction between participants is a point of analysis, a **video recording** is advisable in all

---

4. Regarding the validity of the data, we previously indicated that the researcher always looks for the experience of the respondent with regard to the question at hand. As such he will not be satisfied by general comments which are not linked to a specific person. We previously called this the 'empirical reference'. In the case discussed here, the researcher can apply that maxim but asks respondents to anonymize their story. During the instruction he could indicate either that the story is told from self-experience or from firsthand observation or mention of it by others who experienced it themselves.

cases. The researcher has to ensure he has prior permission from respondents, especially as a video recording is often more threatening than an audio recording.

Finally, we would like to refer to the roles and attitudes of the interviewer as expressed in paragraph 4.5. These apply as well when conducting a focus group. Besides that, the moderator pays additional attention to possible **controversies**; specifically he tries to establish whether the unanimity that is radiated is for real. This implies using the managers' role and active listening by the moderator, while the second observes the body language. Participants can be intimidated, they can feel insufficiently at ease to demonstrate their true opinion, they might not be able to articulate the exact difference between their opinion and experience and that of the others in the group. The moderator might try to facilitate this and enhance *rapport*.

6.6   PHASES IN A FOCUS GROUP

In the previous section we have focused on the points of particular interest in a focus group. In this section we will discuss the phases of a focus group. The following diagram is a diversification of the five phases in the group interview, distinguished by Finch and Lewis (2004:176 ff):

Phases in a focus group

Introduction of the research project
Respondents are welcomed, informal discussions happen. When everyone has arrived, the moderator introduces himself, the second and the research project. He then explains the conversation rules, points to refreshments, explains the sequence of breaks, provides nametags and markers, and asks participants to put their name on the front and back. He then invites people to switch off their mobile telephones and does so himself as well.

Introduction of respondents
The recording device is turned on by the second. The moderator invites respondents to introduce themselves or each other, based on a question he formulated before. Everyone has had the opportunity to speak once, which familiarizes everyone with one another. The moderator might make a drawing with all the names to be put in front of him.

The opening question
The moderator formulates his first main question in such a broad and open way that respondents can answer it from any angle. He indicates that he is interested in everyone's opinion. Probes are kept rather short in this phase; first the whole group should be involved in the interview. The moderator ensures this by relating their answers to each other and inviting others to express their views as well. He notes down key words that he would like to take up later.

'Flow' in the group
If the ice is broken after the initial opening question, the art of moderating is to ensure that the group process continues smoothly, while simultaneously monitoring the contours of discussion. Usually, the moderator has identified a number of themes in advance but he would like to give room to spontaneously emerging themes as well. Silences can be used in this phase to let the group reflect on what was said. The moderator pursues individual statements but he questions the group as a whole on the emerged themes as well. He regularly summarizes what was said to ensure he understood it correctly, as well as inviting participants to supplement issues and building bridges to new themes.

Closure
Based on the predetermined conversation guide, the moderator determines whether all issues have been addressed. The moderator's articulation of the last theme can indicate to participants he is moving towards completion. However, the final question should be an open one; asking whether someone has to add something or forgot to say something. After thanking everyone for their participation, the moderator finishes and the second stops recording. People often like group interviews and, therefore, find it hard to stop. In planning the group, this should be taken into consideration. Sometimes participants also like to linger after the interview is finished.

To conclude this section, we offer some advice per phase.

Opening of the focus group
If a rectangular table is the only one available, it is best for the moderator to sit at either side instead of taking a seat at the head of the table. He ensures the second takes a seat in such a way that eye contact between them is easy and it is possible to signal each other in a manner that is not immediately visible to everyone. The moderator introduces himself and the second and explains the labour division between them briefly. He explains the conversation rules: allow everyone to express their opinion and respect each other even if you disagree, do not get 'personal' in the sense of attacking or insulting other participants. He explains the objective of the study and what will happen to the recording made and the research done. Confidentiality is particularly important. Switch on the recording device.

Introduction of the respondents
He asks respondents to present themselves on the basis of a question he formulated, thereby avoiding possibly sensitive issues in the instruction. He asks them to mention their names prior to introducing themselves for the audio recording.

The starting question
As previously indicated, the starting question should be formulated in such an inviting and open way that participants can choose all kinds of ways to answer, while the contour of the problem remains clear. Everyone is invited to contribute and the moderator tries to create a collective feeling quite soon which enables people to respond to each other. He might mention the possibility of reacting to one another. He tries to avoid probing to deeply in this first round as he would like to ensure that everyone gets involved in the opening question first. He might take some notes on keywords he would like to explore later on, possibly on the map he has drawn earlier, as to know who introduced it.

Flow within the group
At this stage it is important that the group remains active within the contours of the problem statement. Issues are explored; differences checked, new topics are discussed. The moderator has to be quite concentrated; he listens actively, connects aspects, pursues controversies and looks for nuance in the agreement between respondents, sees each opening for a probe, and so on. He handles his conversation guide in a flexible manner. In our experience, themes surface spontaneously if designed properly. The sequence of predefined themes is not fixed; he deviates without worries if the situation develops differently. He moves with the group and monitors both the boundaries of the research problem and time.

Closure
If he thinks all the themes have been sufficiently explored, he completes the interview. If themes are still ongoing but the time has run out, he might propose to the group to continue for a while if he believes all subjects can be completed suf-

ficiently within a reasonable time. If not, he might propose a follow-up session. However, it is advisable to design the conversation guide for the time available and moderate the group accordingly. Slightly extending the session is not always a problem; planning another session can be difficult. In our experience, people like to have a little chat afterwards. It might be useful to allocate some time for this in your schedule.

6.7   ORGANIZATIONAL SKILL AND TALENT IN ORDER TO CREATE THE ART

Similar to Chapter 4, this chapter has covered all sorts of practical and technical matters alongside the Art of interviewing. In particular, the logistics associated with focus groups and designing a good sample are matters that require attention. If the focus group has started, the Art entails to deploy your technical Skill at the right time. Listening actively with all the senses is a first prerequisite to the Art of interviewing, having good working arrangements with the second comes next. Staying calm in such a group and dare to follow it is part of that Art as well. With your 'bottom in the chair' you can still exercise control over what happens but in a relaxed way, offering space to spontaneous group interaction which adds to the richness of the data. Therefore, good preparation is essential. Spend enough time on the design as this will help you to sit back with confidence during the focus group with all your senses wide open. And you'll notice: it is a very enriching experience!

7 | Processing qualitative interviews

In this chapter, we will discuss the processing of qualitative interviews: the recording, filing, transcription, anonymizing and – to a lesser extent – the analysis of them. In the next section we will commence with the recording of interviews.

7.1 Registration of the interview

It is often stated in research proposals that the interview will be **recorded**. Today, this is mostly done digitally. Generally, the recording quality of digital devices is much better than analogue taping devices and they are smaller and easier to transport. The best-known digital recording device is the MP3 player; it is rapidly surpassed by its successor, the MP4 player[1]. An MP3 player records sound directly onto a chip. Often, these devices feature a built-in microphone. However, it is important to check the quality of the microphone in advance, as the recording level can vary between device types. Therefore, we would like to suggest checking the player for the availability of a jack for an external microphone, as this could be useful for focus groups. Normally, a USB cable is included with the MP3 player to transfer the recorded sound to a computer. This only takes a few minutes.

Besides the software, which is supplied together with the recording device to exchange files with a computer, there might be **transcription software** included as well. If so, the only thing the researcher needs to do is install the software and the interview can be transcribed, i.e. written down verbatim, once the audio file is transported to the computer. If there is no transcription software supplied with the device, or the researcher would like to import linked media files with their accompanying transcript into **QDA software**[2], several transcription pro-

---

1. Although we talk about MP3 and MP4 players, the format in which the recording is saved onto the device might vary. It might either be MP3, MP4, WAV, or some format specific for the device, like DSS.
2. QDA software is software, developed for the analysis of Qualitative Data, such as ATLAS.ti, MaxQDA, NVivo. For an overview and comparison between several of these software packages see the special issue of Forum Qualitative Sozialforschung on the KWALON software experiment of January 2011, Vol. 12 no 1: http://www.qualitative-research.net/index.php/fqs/issue/view/36.

grams for digital media files are available on the Internet. In choosing one, it is important to check what kind of audio format the digital recording device uses to record the sound. The most popular **digital audio formats** are MP3, MP4, WAV, OGG, WMA, MSV, and DSS. Which format a file is, can be deciphered from its extension once it is transferred to a computer. Comparable to a Word file which ends with the extension .doc or .docx, the audio file ends with one of the extensions for digital audio format mentioned above. Besides, there are several **video formats** available e.g. MPEG, mov, AVI and WMV[3].

transcription programs[4] aid the researcher in converting sound into text[5]. Mostly, they operate in a fairly simple way while some are more complex. Formerly, most programs only dealt with audio. Today, most of them can deal with either audio or video files, e.g. Express Scribe, f4 and f5. Transcriva, Transana and Transcriber AG in varying degrees offer additional features besides transcription tools for audio and video. Next to those, an additional function is to analyze the transcribed speech in direct relation to the audio or picture file. In this regard Transana has developed itself over time more into a **QDA software**.

These specialized transcription programmes enable the researcher to work in one window where both media file and transcribed text are available. Furthermore, they have specific tools available to lighten the task of transcribing, e.g. 'hot keys' for play, pause, fast forward and fast backward playing of the audio or video file. Another tool is the time loop, mostly set in advance, in which a media fragment will be played for transcription, e.g. a loop of five seconds. This loop will keep rewinding automatically until the typist has transcribed all of it and decides to proceed with the next loop. Other features available in most of these programmes are: variable play back speed, compatibility with a foot pedal and a follow-along mode where the associated fragment gets highlighted in playing the media file.

In typing, the person transcribing finds he has to listen carefully and not to start typing immediately. As we tend to fill in beforehand – in our everyday speech – what we expect others to say, we sometimes do so in transcribing as well. However, people can say things somewhat differently than we would expect them to. For the transcript this is crucial as this needs to be a *verbatim*, i.e. word-by-word, text. **Transcribing** is an intensive and time consuming process; depending on the typing skills of the person transcribing, the researcher allocates four to eight hours transcription time per hour of interview time.

---

3. This list for both audio and video formats is constantly evolving and changing, as developments in digital formats and computers move on.
4. They work on different platforms: some are specifically for either Windows or Mac computers; others are available in separate versions for both platforms.
5. See Evers 2011 for an elaborate description of the influence of technology on transcription and analysis procedures.

In the table below some information on transcription software is provided in alphabetical order[6]. Some of it is available for free on the Internet; others require payment of a (small) fee[7]. As technical information changes rapidly over time, you might want to look up the product website for the latest specifications.

Name of software	Platform	File type[a]	Compatible Formats	Foot pedal support	Playback of video/ audio with high-lighting of asso-ciated text frag-ment (follow along mode)	Synchronous import and playback in QDA software[b]
Express Scribe	Windows Apple OS X	Audio Video	MP3, WAV, WMA, AIFF, MP2, M4A, MSV, DSS, AVI, mov, WMV	Yes	No	No
F4	Windows	Audio Video	All file formats supported by Windows media player[c]	Yes	No	Yes, Atlas.ti and MaxQDA
F5 (same as f4, but different platform)	Apple OS X	Audio Video	All file formats supported by Apple's Quick Time player[c]	Yes	No	Yes, Atlas.ti and MaxQDA
Transana	Windows Apple OS X	Video Audio	MPEG-1, MPEG-2, AVI, mov, WMV, M4V, MP4, MP3,WAV, WMA, and AAC.	Yes[d]	Yes	No
TranscriberAG[e]	Windows XP Apple OS X 10.5 Linux Open-Suse 10.3	Audio Video	WAV, MP3, AU, SPH, AIFF, AIF, FLAC, MP2, OGG, WMA, MPG, MPEG, AVI.	No	Yes	No
Transcriva	Apple OS X	Audio Video	m4a, m4b, m4p, MP3, caf, AIFF, AU, SD2, WAV, SND, AMR, mov, MPEG-4, MPEG-2, MPEG-1, 3GPP, 3GPP2, AVI, DV	Yes	Yes	No

[a] If several file types are supported, the file type for which the software was originally created is mentioned first.

[b] This option lets the QDA software import both transcript and its related media file synchronously and keeps the links between both files – timestamps in transcription software – intact. All the textual files produced in transcription software can be imported into QDA software as a RTF or DOC file, but without the linked media file.

6. Product websites were accessed on May, 23, 2012 for the specifications mentioned in this table.
7. This is changing rapidly: software often begins as *freeware,* and in further development and an acquired reputation, a price has to be paid.

[c] Personal information from dr. Thorsten Dresing, one of the F4/F5 developers.

[d] Under the restriction that the foot pedal can be programmed. Check the products website for further details

[e] Currently works on 32-bit systems only.

If the recording device creates a media format that is not supported by the transcription software intended, the researcher can convert it – using converter software – to one of the formats mentioned in the table. Switch is an audio converter program for both Windows and Apple OS X; Prism is one for converting video.

7.2   ANONYMIZING THE TRANSCRIPT

If all preparatory activities needed to enable the researcher to work on the interview are taken care of, he can start transcribing it. Before doing so, he should determine which **transcription format** he chooses and how he is going to **anonymize the data**. Mostly, respondents were guaranteed confidentiality and privacy, so the transcript should be prepared to show their statements as anonymously as possible[8]. This might be done as follows. In advance, a name for each respondent is decided on. These can be fictitious names: e.g. Thomas, Lloyd or Yvette, a number for every respondent: 1, 2, 3, or a letter in the alphabet for each respondent: A, B, C. In the transcript, they are referred to by that name. During the interview, respondents probably mention others in their immediate surroundings by their name, e.g. their brother John or their daughter Mammate. They might mention names of persons with whom they are connected: e.g. their GP Smith, local policeman Maduro, baker Mulmoz, the street they live in now or lived in earlier: Oxford Street, the hospital they were admitted to: 'when I was in the Charité in Berlin'. They might mention dates: 'that was in 2001, just before September 11', or their age: 'in 1952, when I was two, we moved to Brooklyn'. The researcher might decide to anonymize all these personal references, making the respondent unrecognizable. The simplest form of anonymizing such statements is by replacing them by several dots with or without brackets (...), indicating that something was removed deliberately.[9] Dates, even birthdates, can be changed by adding or subtracting one year if this does not cause contextual problems. If a certain day in a given year is important for the context, e.g. September 11, 2001, then it can be maintained, as it is recognizable to anyone. A birthday can easily be altered by adding or subtracting one day, e.g. April 11, 1954 becomes April 10 or 12, 1954. In this way, dates cannot be traced back to a

---

8. This is important to ensure their anonymity on the researcher's computer as well, in case it gets hacked or is lost.

9. Generally, three dots are used for the omission of one or more sentences and one dot for omitting one or a few words.

specific person. Generally, for the analysis it is not necessary to have such precise information.

It is preferable to design the **anonymizing system** in advance. The researcher designs a name for every respondent and devises a strategy of dealing with recognizable utterances. His notes on this are kept in a separate file or notebook, which is only accessible to him, and he further supplements these notes during transcription. In this file or notebook the fictitious name is stated next to the actual name and possibly the address and so on. He might keep track of how the brother, doctor, etc. are named in the transcript as well, if this is necessary for the research. However, it is crucial that he keeps at least a reminder for the original and fictitious name of every respondent.

7.3   TRANSCRIPTION FORMATS

There are no fixed rules available for transcription of interviews. The choice for a transcription format is associated with the selected analysis method, the available budget and the type of research. Is it fundamental scientific research, aimed at theory construction or is it a type of applied research, aimed at solutions for some practical problem?

For conversation analysis**conversation analysis**, which studies the order of speaking in interaction (Ten Have, 1999:4) a very detailed and elaborate transcription system exists. Every silence is measured and displayed in seconds, as well as the volume of each sound, i.e. raising the voice or emphasis in pronouncing a word or syllable. Some of these symbols are included in the tool buttons of Transana. The key to this method of transcription is that every interaction, interruption, and turn sequence is clear from the textual display, as these are the subject of study in this analysis method. Therefore, it is important that the transcription is as accurate and detailed as possible when displaying the interaction of the conversation. The ?transcription key of Jefferson is used quite often in this type of analysis. See Ten Have (1999:213-214), Silverman (2006:398-399) and Puchta & Potter (2004) for this and other transcription methods.

To illustrate this **Jeffersonian transcription**, a fragment of a relatively simple transcription was taken from Ten Have (2006:18): the beginning of a call. We have literally translated the Dutch in the italic sentences underneath.

0		((telephone rings))
1	A	praktijk dokter↑Noor↓man.
1	A	*Practice of doctor ↑Noor↓man.*
2	C	goedemiddag u spreekt met Van ↑Boor↓de
2	C	*Good afternoon this is Van ↑Boor↓de.*
3		ik heb (.) eh (.) u heeft een ↑brief gekregen,
3		*I have (.) uh (.) you've received a ↑letter,*

4		>als het goed is<
4		>*if that's correct*<
5		van het M O B Prinsen↑gracht (.) eh
5		*from the M O B Prinsen↑gracht (.) uh*
6		over een ↑onderzoek van mijn zoon ↑Bob.
6		*about an ↑examination of my son ↑Bob.*
7	A	ogenblikje.
7	A	one *moment*

The underlining indicates a stress in talk, the arrows a pitch shift in tone, the punctuation marks a more or less falling intonation at the end, the points in brackets a very short break and the > < an increase in speed.

If it is not necessary for analysis in certain research projects to have all these kinds of details available, such as intonation, pauses, overlapping speech, **pragmatic transcription** (Evers 2011) might be used. In this type of transcript, designed by the researcher to fit his analysis needs, everything that is not strictly necessary for the analysis will be omitted, although the rest of the speech will be transcribed verbatim. This might result in transcribing all kinds of repeated utterances, e.g. slips, repetitions, start-ups, confirmations, and stopgaps, i.e. 'uh', 'ah,' 'so', 'anyway', 'and and and', 'yes yes', and 'now' just once, while omitting their repetition from the transcript. On the other hand, silences will not be 'clocked' precisely, as is default in Jeffersonian transcripts but might be represented using a particular symbol, mostly dots in brackets of some sort. The number of dots indicates whether a long-term silence '(…)' or a limited one '(.)' took place but it is not known exactly how long it lasted. For example, one respondent says verbatim:

'If I, if I, if I, I can better articulate this like: if I feel good about myself, everything runs smoother (…). I, I, I like everything better then, everything runs smoothly, you know, right?'

In the transcript might be stated:

'If I, I can better articulate this like: if I feel good about myself, everything runs smoother (…). I like everything better then, everything runs smoothly.'

In addition, there is a transcription format called a **gisted transcript** (Evers 2011) in which during transcription, a selection is made to only transcribe matters which seem relevant to the research question. The next example is taken from Gibbs (2010). All the … indicate omitted text.

'90% of my communication is with … the Sales Director. 1% of his communication is with me. I try to be one step ahead, I get things ready, … because he jumps from one … project to another. … This morning we did Essex, this afternoon we did BT, and we haven't even finished Essex yet.'

For **applied research** specifically the gisted transcript will be used frequently and sometimes, if possible, the pragmatic transcript. If the gisted transcript is used, the researcher makes a selection of statements from the respondent while transcribing. The danger in this approach is that certain matters are 'missing' in the data, as they were omitted during transcription. In our experience, understanding the meaning of data fragments is improved by repetitive reading: in the beginning fragments are overlooked that did not appear to be important at that point. Later on in the analysis, e.g. after analyzing other interviews, it appears that some issues are indeed important for your understanding of something, and suddenly you 'remember' having read this somewhere already. Looking back through interviews, already coded, is then done to check this. In making a selection in advance these discoveries which may prove to be very important, are not possible.

If for some reason the **gisted transcript** or **a summary**[10] is chosen as format, the researcher might consider doing a so called >respondent validation, by submitting the transcript with questions included to the respondent in order to get their agreement with this reproduction of the interview. This can increase the validity of these data.

The readability of the text is improved by using the next format: each speaker has a new line, by using the 'enter' key once, or a blank line, by using the 'enter' key twice[11]. Each speaker can be identified with an initial or a number, if desired in connection with an R for Respondent and I for the Interviewer, e.g. R1 together with I or I1 if more interviewers are working on the project.

If the researcher himself transcribes the audio recording, he might consider placing the **observations or thoughts** with regard to the interview that surface during transcription between brackets **in the transcript**. Square brackets are used to make a distinction between what we have called 'mijn en dijn' elsewhere, or: 'mine and thine' (Evers, 2003). The interpretations and ideas of the researcher should be displayed separately from the actual words, expressions and observed

---

10. In a summary, the recording is not used, even if it is available. The summary is created soon after the interview and tries to reconstruct the interview based on notes taken during the interview and the recollection of the interviewer.
11. Which option is preferred depends on both the interview structure and the analysis. If the interview is done in quite a structured way, with little room for dwelling and answers are – kept – short, a blank line can facilitate automated searching and coding. If there is room for elaboration, auto-coding is not advisable.

behaviour of the respondent. While analyzing with QDA-software, such as AT-LAS.ti, MAXQda, or NVivo, these thoughts and observations can be transferred from the transcript into annotation tools[12] and 'linked' to the actual spot in the interview transcript to display them separately.

The task of transcribing could be outsourced to a **professional transcriber** who sometimes works faster. It is important that the researcher checks the transcript afterwards to ensure it is a verbatim account of what was said during the interview. Even in transcribing, it sometimes occurs that the spoken word is 'interpreted', that is, unnoticed or unconsciously text is produced which is close to what was said, but yet not verbatim.

We have developed an **instruction for transcription,** used by the transcriber in one of our research projects:

> Here is a fictitious transcript, in which the words in italics could have been omitted in the transcript. The underlined words are in-between cases, because they can either indicate a repetition, a reaffirmation or reinforcement. This can often be discerned from the tone of voice, so listen carefully. If in doubt, always include it in the transcript!

> I: *uh, uh,* I wanted to ask you: How do you think about this job?
> R: *Yes,* what do I think of this job … that's a difficult question, *be be be because* because I must think about that. I think it's a very nice environment, yes, a very nice environment. Great colleagues, interesting work, etc.. The building is so-so, but ok, you can't have everything, do you now?
> I: Could you elaborate a bit on….. what do you mean by: great colleagues?
> R: What do I mean by great colleagues?
> I: Yes.
> R: *Yes,* what do I mean with that. People, who are warm-hearted, enjoy their work; don't mind rolling up their sleeves and occasionally help each other out if that's convenient.
> I: What do you mean by help each other out ? In what way?
> R: Well, for example, if you need to get something done and time runs short, your colleague will help you out. Or if your colleague has knowledge which might be important or interesting for your work, he will share it.
> I: *Yes yes.* Those things you just described, do your colleagues here do all that?
> R: Most will, yes indeed, that's the culture around here.
> I: Can you tell me what type of content makes your job interesting to you? So, I mean, *what's interesting content?*

7.4   STORING DATA

If much data is collected, a **data storing system** should be developed in advance, in which both data files and the project file, which is created within QDA-software[13] are kept on a computer. This might mean that certain folders are created in which to organize the data[14], e.g. according to their file type, textual files versus audio files, or resembling the collection method, i.e. interviews versus fieldnotes. The entire project with all its associated files, including the raw data files, i.e. the transcribed interviews, are kept both on a computer and on a different carrier, e.g. an external hard disk, USB stick or CD-ROM. If a type QDA software is used, which either includes the raw material in the software project file, e.g. NVivo, or manages it from within the software, e.g. ATLAS.ti 7, we recommend saving the raw data files separately as well. It is important to save everything in two places because something might go wrong on a computer. Text can disappear accidentally, the researcher makes notes he later wishes to remove, something goes wrong in entering the data into the QDA software, and so on. Having kept everything in separate places and perhaps the raw data files in a separate place as well enables the researcher to fall back on the back up files if something happens to the original. This **file archive** is kept for emergency purposes.

7.5   USING SOFTWARE FOR QUALITATIVE DATA ANALYSIS

Once – part of – the data are transcribed the next step in the research process, the **data analysis**, can begin. There are several ways to analyze qualitative data. We will not discuss them in this book; suffice to refer to Boeije (2005b), Coffey and Atkinson (1996), Grbich (2007), di Gregorio and Davidson (2008), Saldaña (2009), Friese (2012), Bazeley (2007) and Wester and Peters (2004). They discuss several ways of analyzing qualitative data.

As was stated earlier, **QDA software** can be used to analyze the data. The acronym **CAQDAS** was developed for this purpose: Computer Assisted Qualitative Data Analysis. Several software packages are available, sometimes as shareware or freeware like Cassandre[15], which supports the analysis of research data. In the Netherlands, especially the packages ATLAS.ti, Kwalitan, MAXQDA and NVivo

---

13. We assume that the researcher as a default will use QDA software. In our experience, the advantages in doing so are quite considerable if compared with the manual work done before. Not only is it far easier and faster to query the dataset once it has been coded, so more questions will be put to the data, but also the whole process of analysis is far more traceable and all project related matters are in one file which makes the project surveyable.

14. This will only apply if the QDA software approaches the data files separately (ATLAS.ti 5 and 6), instead of embedding them (NVivo) or copying the whole data set into a separate folder which is managed by the QDA software (ATLAS.ti 7).

15. See Lejeune (2011) on the use of Cassandre.

are used. Besides these, Transana, Dedoose and QDA Miner are some packages developed for this purpose. See the special issue of Forum Qualitative Social Research regarding the KWALON experiment with QDA software (Evers, Silver, Mruck and Peeters, 2011), diGregorio & Davidson (2008) and Lewins & Silver (2007) for a comparison of a number of programmes and their functionality.

This **QDA-software** is more functional than a mere supporting analysis; they simultaneously trace what is done and as such act as an accounting device for the entire research project. Anything previously written and preserved on yellow post-it-notes will now be saved as memos within the project file. Therefore, it is useful to use QDA-software right from the start of the research project; the first thoughts concerning the project can be noted in the project file. All these packages contain a special tool, the **memo**, in which the researcher keeps track of his thoughts and ideas, as well as documenting the entire research process. Several types of memos can be created, e.g. concerning process descriptions, methodological choices, theory formation, the research design, and literature description to name a few. These memos are then used during the reporting phase to reconstruct the line of thought during the project, to justify theoretical insights gained and to show the decision process within the study. It provides insight into the research and makes it transparent, thus contributing to the reliability of it.

Besides memos, **codes**[16] are an important other tool within these computer programs. It is quite easy in QDA software to separate the data into smaller chunks and code them. Next, all fragments which are coded with a particular code can be retrieved quite simply which allows comparing them to verify if they mean the same. In addition, these programmes have many other analysis tools such as the ability to visualize relationships between concepts or to illustrate the relationships between data fragments. However, it is beyond the aim of this book to discuss the use of QDA software or qualitative analysis in-depth.

7.6   TECHNOLOGY TO SUPPORT THE ART

This chapter focused on technical features that might support the research project and increase its reliability and validity. The use of QDA software, for instance, might save some time. We argue that you should make use of such tools whenever possible, let technology work for you! Realize though, that technology does not make your Skill redundant; you will still have to carry out the quality check and put your Art to work in order to be able make a creative and responsible analysis.

---

16. Keywords, typifying snippets of data.

Appendix

Appendix I. Reflection checklist[1]

Reflection on the introduction to the interview
1. Was the introduction clear enough for the respondent or gatekeeper? Did he comprehend the purpose of the research project easily?
2. How did you react to doubt or questions from the potential respondent? Was it:
   - Empathic enough? Did you give them enough space?
   - Clarifying?
   - Underpinning the importance of their collaboration in your project?
   - Meticulous, both using correct language as in listening actively?
3. Was it obvious to them that you have put sufficient preparation in the subject and the social world of the respondent to be relevant for them?
4. Did you sufficiently underpin the interest the research might have for them?

Reflection on interview techniques
In every main question, summaries, probes and follow-up question are used in continuous alternation. To reflect on the quality of your interview you might consider the following points.

Reflection on summaries:
1. Are your summaries correct?
   - Given in your own words?
   - Is the non-verbal behaviour included in them?
2. Is the summary open enough?
   - Is your summary such that the respondent feels he can correct it? You might do this for instance by starting your summary with: 'If I understand correctly ...' and ending it in an inviting tone.
   - Are you inviting the respondent to comment on it?
3. Are you summarizing sufficiently?
   - Are summaries used to structure the interview?
   - Are summaries used as a checking device: to check whether you understood the respondent correctly?
   - Are summaries used to establish rapport?

---

1. Adaptation from Maso 2003, Appendix 4.

Reflection on your probes and follow up questions
1. Are questions follow-up questions or are they probes?
2. What kind of follow-up questions do you use and what techniques are used to probe?
   a. Repeating the answer
   b. Asking to clarify what is meant by:
      • A certain word or
      • A (part of) a statement
   c. Asking the respondent to elaborate on a certain statement
   d. Inquiring about certain aspects of non-verbal behaviour you observed
   e. Introducing silences and inviting them non-verbally, with your glance or by nodding, to elaborate
   f. Summarizing your question and the answer(s) given by the respondent
   g. Confronting: contrasting a statement by the respondent with another statement or summary
3. Are your follow-up questions diversified?
4. Did you use all the types of probes mentioned?
5. Did you explore the topic sufficiently, i.e. did you learn all there is to learn by probing sufficiently?
6. Are your probes and follow-up questions formulated in a neutral sense?
   Do not start the question with words like 'But....' or 'Yes, but....', as this might suggest that you disagree or that you think the respondent's answer is odd.
7. Are you formulating 'your own' questions during the interview?
   In using the Opening-the-locks model, you only use probes, while in using the River model, you use probes and follow-up questions. The latter should build on themes suggested by the respondent earlier.
8. Are you evading certain questions because you think they might be painful or unpleasant to the respondent?
   Mostly, it will be you who is having some difficulty with that question.
9. Did you include the respondent's non-verbal behaviour in your questioning line, either in probes or follow-up questions?
10. Did you encourage respondents in your focus group to talk to each other? Did all respondents in the group participate sufficiently?

Reflection on your attitude
1. Is your attitude towards the respondent genuinely interested, open and accepting?
2. If you do not comprehend an answer immediately, do you let the respondent know with your non-verbal behaviour? Can you empathize with the respondent? Do you use glances of non-comprehension?
3. Is your verbal and non-verbal behaviour adapted to the respondent?

4. Do you discuss one of the following situations with the respondent if they occur?
   - You are annoyed by the respondent or feel a strong antipathy or attraction, which is causing you to not function properly
   - You do not agree with the respondent's story, or you do not believe it
   - Disturbances, noise, or other people present are influencing the interview in a negative way
   - Some private matters are bothering you and they influence the interview negatively.
5. Did the teamwork with the second in a focus group function satisfactorily to you both? Did you have enough eyes for his messages during the interview?

APPENDIX II. LIST OF CORE CONCEPTS

Account: the respondent offers self-defensive explanations for unacceptable behaviour, thus hoping to make it socially acceptable.

Active listening: Active listening not only implies the interviewer hears what is being said; he also puts himself in the position of his respondent, i.e. comprehend what he is saying and translate its possible implications back to his problem statement. This latter act of translation is termed: thinking along analytically.

Bias: is the prejudice of the researcher which distorts his perception. Bias may include preconceptions about others, which everyone has, but it can also be facilitated by a particular view of science or the literature used for the project which may be reasoning in a certain direction.

Bracketing: placing your own experience and premises as a person, interviewer or researcher, between brackets in trying to question the respondent as openly as possible, as if his experience is totally new to you.

Coding: attaching one or more key words to fragments of data. These key words, or codes, indicate the content of the fragment or the interpretation of it by the researcher. Codes can be used in many different ways, depending on the type of analysis. In QDA software, coding means linking one code to some fragment, enabling the researcher to search their data quite easily and as such getting an overview of the dataset.

Conceptual model: a visual reproduction of the most important themes and concepts and their mutual relationships, which the researcher would like to investigate. It is an aid in formulating what is important in the research project and as such a visual representation of the theoretical framework.

Conversation guide: a list of themes or questions the researcher would like to pose during the interview. It can differentiate between a list of key words and a detailed list of questions which even might be provided with a time schedule.

Deduction: the researcher departs from an existing theory, derives one or more hypotheses from it, collects the necessary data and verifies if these data can confirm the theory. Often this method is associated with quantitative research in which hypotheses will be tested through statistical procedures. However, in qualitative research hypotheses are being used more frequently as well. Deduction moves from theory towards the empirical world.

Elicitation techniques: Elicitation techniques are specific ways of interrogating or the use of specific aids. They are used to motivate respondents to provide information. They differ from normal methods of questioning because an additional stimulus is applied within the question or a tool such as a photograph, a picture or an assignment is used to get specific information.

Empirical research: indicates systematic observations, whether or not done through the senses, in the empirical or social reality, or a reproduction of them. In qualitative research it is common to gather information on a phenomenon in its natural surroundings.

Epistemology: the theory of knowledge: What is the essence of knowledge, how is it attained and what are its limits? In short: what reason can we have for a certain conviction or why do we believe in something?

Fieldnotes: notes taken while observing in the natural setting of respondents. Thereby, so-called jottings are done in key words which will be written out later in descriptive fieldnotes. These are elaborated reports of what was observed, heard and smelled, joined with the thoughts, ideas or premises the researcher has on all this. These descriptive fieldnotes are sometimes elaborated with drawings, maps and other visual means to clarify matters further. These descriptive fieldnotes and their visual means together form the dataset which will be analyzed.

Flow in the interview: the interview is following a smooth track in which there is room for silences, while the stream of thoughts that is triggered by the interview in both interviewer and interviewee is balanced. The interviewer adapts his behaviour and stream of thoughts to that of the interviewee and keeps his own line of thought, to which he would like to refer to at a later point, separated by jotting it down in key words.

Focus group: a group of six to ten respondents who will be questioned on the research topic. Respondents are selected and put into several groups with shared characteristics, e.g. sex, income, profession, hobby, the researcher thinks are relevant to the research topic. If he differentiates respondents according to some background characteristic(s), this is termed 'segmentation'.

Front: the respondent is trying to emphasize his image by exaggerating his role.

Gatekeeper: person that determines access to potential respondents. For example, this might be a secretary in an organization if the manager is to be interviewed, members of a board of directors if employees are to be interviewed, committee members if the members of their association are to be interviewed, parents if children are to be interviewed, or doctors if patients are to be interviewed.

Going native: The researcher is trying very hard to be part of the group he investigates; he denies his own background and identity. The result is that he is not listening, watching and analysing critically enough.

Individual interview: interview in which one or two respondents are questioned on the topic of research.

Induction: empirical data are used to construct a theory about the social world. The broad information which was collected in the field is the groundwork to reach a specific image of the context, with a matching classification, typology or some core category. Induction moves from empirical world towards theory.

Informant: a person, very familiar with the research target group. He mostly has a transcending and advisory role in the research project and is sometimes referred to as a key respondent or key informant.

Internal reliability: in short, this refers to the project being done in a consistent and logical manner, while team members, if applicable, agree on the interpretation of concepts and results and apply these consistently.

Internal validity: in short, this refers to interviewer and respondent talking about the same matters which coincide with the topic being researched. The research results should be based on a sound research design, the use of applicable methods, and techniques of research, as well as a sound analysis of data.

Memo: tool in QDA software to record thoughts, ideas, premises, hypotheses, preliminary results, analysis steps and summaries of the literature review. Memos might be typified as theoretical, logs, methodical, analytical and so on. During the research project, they will change from concrete process descriptions into theorizing and more abstract.

Method: the working procedure adopted in a research project. This might entail a certain data collection method, i.e. interviewing or participant observation, a collection of techniques inspired by a certain approach, i.e. ethnography, case study or biographical research, or a certain analysis strategy, i.e. grounded theory analysis, metaphor analysis or argumentation analysis.

Methodology: the underlying logic and theoretical assumptions which guide a research project.

Ontology: the theory of being; it deals with the general properties of matters, for example the view that observable reality is independent of human knowledge.

Operationalization: the refashioning of an abstract concept into one which can be investigated or observed in the empirical world.

Paradigm: a paradigm frames a research project because it defines the way research should be done. It is primarily 'an exemplary, normative example' that indicates which kind of problem has to be investigated and how this should be done. This can only be learned under supervision of experienced persons.

Participant observation: a type of data collection stemming from cultural anthropology in which the researcher participates in the everyday life of his subjects and captures his observations in jottings and descriptive field notes which are the foundation for analysis.

Qualitative interview: A qualitative interview is a form of information gathering in which the interviewer queries one or more respondents based on a research question. Thereby, the interviewer creates space for the respondents to dwell – in their own words – on the perceived facts, their experiences, the meaning they give to the subject of investigation, nuances regarding it and its possible effect on their lives. In doing so, the interviewer tries to understand and thoroughly investigate the respondents' world.

Rapport: the trusting relationship that develops between the interviewer and the respondent. Initially, it is the task of the interviewer to ensure conditions for this are present, but it is obviously a matter of reciprocity whether it will succeed. It is generally accepted that there has to be sufficient *rapport* for a good exchange of information, in which the respondent feels safe enough to share more sensitive issues with the interviewer.

Reliability: In internal reliability, members of the research team agree intersubjectively on the interpretation of concepts and results and these are used in a consistent manner. To enhance external reliability, the researcher works in his project consistently, logically and traceably as to enable others to virtually repeat the project with comparable results

Resistance: if there is resistance amongst a respondent he does not really want to be present or participate in the interview. This will generally be expressed in the form of muttered phrases or minor behavioural gestures. If resistance is observed, we advise you to discuss this before proceeding with the interview.

Respondent: the person a researcher would like to interview for his research project.

Sample: total number of persons the researcher wishes to approach for his project. In qualitative research mostly a purposeful sample is used based on determined selection via background characteristics as opposed to probability selection in which everybody has an equal chance.

Theoretical frame(work): the literature review, previously done in designing a research project. Mostly a conceptual model will be distilled from this review to guide the project.

Thinking along analytically: during the interview the information gathered is related to the problem statement, mutual relationships between items of obtained information are identified, the accuracy of these is checked with the respondent and it is assessed whether the information has been explored sufficiently deep to answer the question.

Validity: Internal validity means the interviewer and the respondent talk about the same thing and that the topic discussed is in accordance with the problem statement. External validity is the extent to which the results of the project can be extrapolated to other groups of people, situations or places. In short, the generalizability of the results.

Bibliography

Abma, T.A. (1996). *Responsief evalueren. Discoursen, controversen en allianties in het postmoderne.* Delft: Eburon (dissertation).

Abma, T.A. (2002). Verhalen in dialoog. Een narratief organisatieonderzoek op een dansacademie en conservatorium. *Tijdschrift voor Humanistiek*, vol. 3, nr. 11, pp. 9-24.

Adler, P.A. & P. Adler (2002). The Reluctant Respondent. In: J.F. Gubrium & J.A. Holstein (eds.), *Handbook of Interview Research. Context and Method.* Thousand Oaks: Sage, pp. 515-536.

Baakman, Nico A.A. (2007) Het elite-interview als sociale opgave. In: Jeanine Evers (ed.) *Kwalitatief interviewen: kunst én kunde,* pp. 201-214. Den Haag: Lemma.

Baarda, D.B., M.P.M. de Goede & A.G.E. van der Meer-Middelburg (1996). *Open interviewen. Praktische handleiding voor het voorbereiden en afnemen van open interviews.* Groningen: Stenfert Kroese.

Baart, A. (2002). *Training exploratief interview. Cursusmateriaal voor het aanleren van het explorerende (diepte)interview in kwalitatief onderzoek. Deel cursisten.* Utrecht: Katholieke Theologische Universiteit, 2nd version.

Babbie, Earl (2004). *The Practice of Social Research.* Belmont, CA: Wadsworth/Thomson Learning. 10th Edition.

Bazeley, Pat (2007). *Qualitative Data Analysis with NVivo.* London: Sage.

Beekman, T. & K. Mulderij (1983). *Beleving en ervaring. Werkboek fenomenologie voor de sociale wetenschappen.* Amsterdam: Boom.

Bennamar, K. et al. (2006). *Reflectietools.* Den Haag: LEMMA.

Bernard, H. Russel (2006). *Research Methods in Anthropology. Qualitative and Quantitative Approaches.* Lanham: Altamira Press. Fourth Edition.

Boeije, H. (2005a). Interviewen in de aanwezigheid van een derde persoon. In: F. Wester, H. Boeije & T. Hak (ed.), *Methodische keuzen in kwalitatief onderzoek. KWALON 30,* vol. 10, nr. 3, pp. 35-49.

Boeije, H. (2005b). *Analyseren in kwalitatief onderzoek. Denken en doen.* Amsterdam: Boom Onderwijs.

Boeije, Hennie (2010). *Analysis in Qualitative Research.* London: Sage.

Boeije, Hennie, Harm 't Hart en Joop Hox (2009) (red.). *Onderzoeksmethoden.* Boom Onderwijs.

Boer, F. de (1994). *De interpretaties van het verschil. De vertaling van klachten van mannen en vrouwen in de Riagg.* Amsterdam: Het Spinhuis.

Bogdan, R.C. & S. Knopp Biklen (2007). *Qualitative Research for Education. An introduction to Theories and Methods.* Boston: Person Education.

Bogdan, Robert & Steven J. Taylor (1975). *Introduction to Qualitative Research Methods. A Phenomenological Approach to the Social Sciences.* New York: John Wiley & Sons

Bogner, Alexander, Beate Littig & Wolfgang Menz (Hrsg.) *Experteninterviews. Theorien, Methoden, An-weldungsfelder*. Wiesbaden: VS Verlag. 3., grundlegend überarbeitete Auflage.

Booth, T. & W. Booth (2003, orig. 1994). The Use of Depth Interviewing with Vulnerable Subjects: Lessons from a Research Study of Parents with Learning Dissa-bilities. In: N. Fielding, *Interviewing. Volume IV. Sage Benchmarks in Social Research Methods*. London: Sage, pp. 15-33.

Borgatti, S.P. (1999). Elicitation Techniques for Cultural Domain Analysis. In: J.J. Schensul, M.D. LeCompte, B.K. Nastasi & S.P. Borgatti, *Enhanced Ethnographic Methods. Audiovisual Techniques, Focused Group Interviews, and Elicitation Techniques. Ethnographer's Toolkit part 3*. Walnut Creek: Altamira Press, pp. 115-151.

Braam, S. (2003). *Tussen gekken & gajes. Avonturen in de undercoverjournalistiek*. Amsterdam: Nijgh & Van Ditmar.

Braster, J.F.A. (2000). *De kern van casestudy's*. Assen: Van Gorcum.

Bryman, Alan (ed.) (2001). *Ethnography. Volumes I-IV. Sage Benchmarks in Research Methods*. London: Sage

Bryman, A. (2004). *Social Research Methods*. Oxford: Oxford University Press.

Coffey, A. & P. Atkinson (1996). *Making Sense of Qualitative Data. Complementary Research Strategies*. Thousand Oaks: Sage.

Craig, E. (2002). *De kortste introductie filosofie*. Utrecht: Het Spectrum BV.

Crane, J.G. & M.V. Angrosino (1992). *Field projects in anthropology. A student handbook*. Illinois: Waveland Press Inc.

Creswell, J.W. (2007). *Qualitative Inquiry and Research Design. Choosing Among Five Traditions*. 2nd Edition. Thousand Oaks: Sage.

Cummins, R.A. (2002). Proxy Responding for Subjective Well-Being: A Review. *International Review of Research in Mental Retardation*, vol. 25, pp. 183-207.

Dey, Ian (2005, orig. 1993) *Qualitative Data Analysis. A User-Friendly Guide for Social Scientists*. London: Routledge.

Ellis, C.N., Ch.E. Kiesinger & L.M. Tillmann-Healy (1997). Interactive Interviewing. Talking About Emotional Experience. In: Rosanna Hertz (ed.), *Reflexivity and Voice*. Thousand Oakes: Sage, pp. 119-149.

Emans, Ben (2002) *Interviewen. Theorie, techniek en training*. Groningen: Stenfert Kroese. 4th edition

Emmerson, Robert M., Rachel I. Fretz & Linda L. Shaw (1995) *Writing Ethnographic Fieldnotes*. Chicago: Chicago University Press

Evers, J. (2001). *Instituties op Curaçao: een politiek-bestuurlijke analyse. Kada felt di flor tin sumpiña*. Rotterdam: Erasmus Universiteit (thesis Public Administration).

Evers, J. (2003). Ethische professionaliteit in de rapportage. In: F. Wester (red.), *Rapporteren over kwalitatief onderzoek*. Utrecht: LEMMA, pp. 99-128.

Evers, J. (2004a). Interviewen, interviewen, interviewen. Twee megapublicaties over interviewen. *KWALON 25*, vol. 9, nr. 1, pp. 56-65.

Evers, J. (2004b). Bereiken en verstaan bij het tienjarig bestaan van het Verwey-Jonker Instituut. *KWALON 25*, vol. 9, nr. 1, pp. 76-79.

Evers, Jeanine (2007). (ed.) *Kwalitatief interviewen: kunst én kunde.* Den Haag: Boom/Lemma.

Evers, Jeanine C. and AnneLoes van Staa (2010) *Qualitative Analysis in a Case Study.* In: Albert J. Mills, Gabrielle Durepos and Elden Wiebe (eds.) *Encyclopedia of Case Study Research*, pp. 747-759.

Evers, Jeanine C. (2011). From the Past into the Future. How Technological Developments Change Our Ways of Data Collection, Transcription and Analysis. *Forum Qualitative Sozialforschung / Forum Qualitative Social Research*, 12(1), Art. 38, http://nbn-resolving.de/urn:nbn:de:0114-fqs1101381.

Fessem, Ad van (2007) Focusgroepen in marktonderzoek. In: Jeanine Evers (ed.) *Kwalitatief interviewen: kunst én kunde*, pp. 139-150. Den Haag: Lemma.

Fielding, Nigel (ed.) (2003). *Interviewing. Volume I-IV. Sage Benchmarks in Social Research Methods.* London: Sage

Finch, H. & J. Lewis (2004). Focus Groups. In: Jane Ritchie & Jane Lewis (eds.). *Qualitative Research Practice. A Guide for Social Science Students and Researchers.* London: Sage, pp. 170-198.

Fine, M. (1994). Working the Hyphens. Reinventing Self and Other in Qualitative Research. In: N. Denzin & Y.S. Lincoln (eds.), *Handbook of Qualitative Research*, pp. 70-82.

Friese, Susanne (2012). *Qualitative Data Analysis with Atlas.ti.* London: Sage

Frissen, P.H.A. (1996). *De virtuele staat. Politiek, bestuur, technologie.* Schoonhoven: Academic Service.

Geertz, C. (1973). *The Interpretation of Cultures.* New York: Basic Books.

Gemert, Frank van (2007) Daders op vrije voeten. Etnografisch veldwerk van een criminoloog. In: Jeanine Evers (ed.) *Kwalitatief interviewen: kunst én kunde,* pp. 151-160. Den Haag: Lemma.

Gibbs, G. (2010). *Two short videos of lectures on issues of transcription,* Part 1 and 2, (http://onlineqda.hud.ac.uk/movies/transcription/index.php [Accessed: May 25, 2012]

Gier, E. de, J. Evers, P. de Jong & L. Sterckx (2001). *Wetenschap: roeping of beroep. Verslag van een verkennend onderzoek naar de (on)aantrekkelijkheid van een loopbaan in wetenschappelijk onderzoek.* Zoetermeer: Ministerie van OCenW. Beleidsgerichte studies HO & WO, nr. 76.

Giorgi, A. (1994). A phenomenological perspective on certain qualitative research methods. *Journal of Phenomenological Psychology*, vol. 25, nr. 2, pp. 207.

Gold (1969) Roles in Sociological Field Observations. In: George J. McCall & J.L. Simmons (eds.) *Issues in Participant Observation. A Text and Reader.* Reading: Addison-Wesley Publishing Company

Gorden, R.L. (1998). *Basic Interviewing Skills.* Illinois: Waveland Press.

Gorden, R.L. (2003, orig. 1956). Dimensions of the Depth Interview. In: N. Fielding, *Interviewing. Volume I. Sage Benchmarks in Social Research Methods.* London: Sage, pp. 170-179.

Grbich, C. (1999). *Qualitative Research in Health. An Introduction.* London: Sage.

Grbich, C. (2007). *Qualitative data analysis. An introduction.* London: Sage.

Gregorio, Silvana di & Judith Davidson (2008). *Qualitative Research Design for Software Users.* Maidenhead: Open University Press McGraw-Hill

Hampsink, Monique & Nanette Hagedoorn (2006). *Beweging in je brein. Zestig werkvormen voor inspirerende trainingen, workshops en presentaties.* Den Haag: Academic Service/Sdu Uitgevers bv

Hart, H. 't, H. Boeije & J. Hox (red.) (2005). *Onderzoeksmethoden.* Amsterdam: Boom Onderwijs.

Have, P. ten (1999). *Doing Conversational Analysis. A Practical Guide.* London: Sage.

Have, P. ten (2006). Conversatieanalyse: orde in de details. *KWALON 32*, vol. 11, nr. 2, pp. 16-23.

Heaton, Janet (2004). *Reworking Qualitative Data.* London: Sage

Heldens, J. & F. Reysoo (2005). De kunst van het interviewen: reflecties op het interview met een *guide.* In: F. Wester, H. Boeije & T. Hak (red.), *Methodische keuzen in kwalitatief onderzoek. KWALON 30*, vol. 10, nr. 3, pp. 106-121.

Holloway I. & S. Wheeler (2002). *Qualitative Research in Nursing.* Oxford: Blackwell Science.

Hollway, W. & T. Jefferson (2003, orig. 1997). Eliciting Narrative through the In-Depth Interview. In: N. Fielding, *Interviewing. Volume II. Sage Benchmarks in Social Research Methods.* London: Sage, pp. 170-179.

Jaffe, R. (2005). Repertory grid and sentence completion: twee kwalitatieve methoden in de Caraïbische praktijk. *KWALON 29*, vol. 10, nr. 2, pp. 22-29.

Jedeloo, S. et al. (2006). *Preferenties van chronisch zieke adolescente zorggebruikers: vier profielen. Een Q-methodologisch onderzoek onder chronisch zieke jongeren van het Erasmus M–Sophia in de leeftijd van 12 tot 19 jaar.* Rotterdam: Project Op Eigen Benen, Hogeschool Rotterdam, rapport 3.

Johnson, J.M. (2002). In-Depth Interviewing. In: J.F. Gubrium & J.A. Holstein, *Handbook of Interview Research. Context and Method.* Thousand Oaks: Sage, pp. 103-119.

Johnson, J.C. & S.C. Weller (2002). Elicitation Techniques for Interviewing. In: J.F. Gubrium & J.A. Holstein, *Handbook of Interview Research. Context and Method.* Thousand Oaks: Sage, pp. 491-514.

Jonker, E. (2007). Vriendschap als leidraad. Vragen naar levensverhalen in interviews. In: Jeanine Evers (ed.) *Kwalitatief interviewen: kunst én kunde*, pp. 161-174 Den Haag: Lemma.

Keken, H. van (2006). *Voor het onderzoek. Het formuleren van de probleemstelling.* Amsterdam: Boom Onderwijs.

Kelle, U., G. Prein & K. Bird (eds.) (1998). *Computer-aided Qualitative Data Analysis. Theory, Methods and Practice.* London: Sage.

Kitzinger, J. (2003, orig. 1994) The Methodology of Focus Groups: The Importance of Interaction Between Research Participants. In: N. Fielding, *Interviewing. Volume I. Sage Benchmarks in Social Research Methods.* London: Sage, pp. 347-364.

Kloos, P. (1981). *Culturele antropologie.* Assen: Van Gorcum.

Kröber, Hans R.Th. en Jeroen Zomerplaag (2007) Mensen met een verstandelijke beperking betrekken bij onderzoek. Een kritisch emancipatoir perspectief. In: Jeanine Evers (ed.) *Kwalitatief interviewen: kunst én kunde*, pp. 215-224. Den Haag: Lemma.

Krueger, R.A. (1998). *Moderating Focus Groups. Focus Group Kit 4.* Thousand Oakes: Sage.

Kuijlman W. & N. Bos-Schous (2006). *Practicum interview- en observatietraining.* Utrecht: Universiteit voor Humanistiek, werkboek Ba1.

Lange, Jacomine de (2007) Interviewen van ouderen. Enkele praktische tips. In: Jeanine Evers (ed.) *Kwalitatief interviewen: kunst én kunde,* pp. 225-232. Den Haag: Lemma.

Laslett, B. & R. Rapoport (2003, orig. 1975). Collaborative Interviewing and Interactive Research. In: N. Fielding, *Interviewing. Volume III. Sage Benchmarks in Social Research Methods.* London: Sage, pp. 74-87.

LeCompte, M.D. & J.J. Schensul (1999). *Analyzing & Interpreting Ethnographic Data.* Walnut Creek: Altamira Press, vol. 5 van de 'Ethnographer's Toolkit'.

Legard, R., J. Keegan & K. Ward (2004). In-depth Interviews. In: J. Ritchie & J. Lewis (eds.), *Qualitative Research Practice. A Guide for Social Science Students and Research-ers*. London: Sage, pp. 138-169.

Lejeune, Christophe (2011). From Normal Business to Financial Crisis…and Back Again. An Illustration of the Benefits of *Cassandre* for Qualitative Analysis. In: *Forum Qualitative Sozialforschung / Forum: Qualitative Social Research, (12)*1, Art. 24.

Lewins, A. & Ch. Silver (2007). *Using Software in Qualitative Research. A step-by-step Guide*. London: Sage.

Lewis, J. (2004). Design Issues. In: J. Ritchie & J. Lewis (eds.), *Qualitative Research Practice. A Guide for Social Science Students and Researchers*. London: Sage, pp. 47-76.

Liempt, Ilse van (2007) 'Secrets and lies': interviewervaringen met gesmokkelde migranten in Nederland. In: In: Jeanine Evers (ed.) *Kwalitatief interviewen: kunst én kunde,* pp. 233-242. Den Haag: Lemma.

Maanen, J. van & S.R. Barley (1985) Cultural Organization: Fragments of a Theory. In: P.J. Frost et al. (eds.), *Organizational Culture.* Beverly Hills/London: Sage, pp. 31-54

Mann, Ch. & F. Stewart (2002). Internet Interviewing. In: J.F. Gubrium & J.A. Holstein, *Handbook of Interview Research. Context and Method.* Thousand Oaks: Sage, pp. 603-627.

Maso, I. (2002). Phenomenology and Ethnography. In: P. Atkinson et al. (eds.), *Handbook of Ethnography.* London: Sage, pp. 136-144.

Maso, I. (2006). Het open interview. In: W. Kuijlman & N. Bos-Schous, *Practicum Interview- en observatietraining.* Utrecht: Werkboek Universiteit voor Humanistiek, pp. 12-21.

Maso, I. & A. Smaling (2004, orig. 1998). *Kwalitatief onderzoek: praktijk en theorie.* Amsterdam: Boom.

Maso (2007) Het hermeutische interview. In: Jeanine Evers (ed.) *Kwalitatief interviewen: kunst én kunde,* pp. 175-184. Den Haag: Lemma.

Merton, R.K. (2003, orig. 1987). The Focussed Interview and Focus Groups: Continuities and Discontinuities. In: N. Fielding, *Interviewing. Volume I. Sage Benchmarks in Social Research Methods.* London: Sage, pp. 261-276.

Merton, R.K., M. Fiske & P.L. Kendall (1990, orig. 1956). *The Focused Interview. A Manual of Problems and Procedures.* New York: The Free Press.

Merton, R.K. & P.L. Kendall (2003, orig. 1946). The Focused Interview. In: N. Fielding, *Interviewing. Volume I. Sage Benchmarks in Social Research Methods.* London: Sage, pp. 232-260.

Mey, Günter & Katja Mruck (Hrsg.) (2010). *Handbuch Qualitative Forschung in der Psychologie.* Wiesbaden: VS Verlag

Miles, M.B. & A.M. Huberman (1994). Qualitative Data Analysis. An Expanded Source-book, Thousand Oaks: Sage.

Morgan, D.L. (1988). *Focus Groups as Qualitative Research. Qualitative Research Methods, Volume 16.* Newbury Park: Sage.

Morgan, D.L. (1998a). *The Focus Group Guidebook. Focus Group Kit 1.* Thousand Oakes: Sage.

Morgan, D.L. (1998b). *Planning Focus Groups. Focus Group Kit 2.* Thousand Oakes: Sage.

Morgan, D.L. (2003, orig. 1996). Focus Groups. In: N. Fielding, *Interviewing. Volume I. Sage Benchmarks in Social Research Methods.* London: Sage, pp. 323-346.

Mulderij, K.J. (1999). Waarschuwing: dreigend overschot! Over te veel methode in de jaren negentig. In: B. Levering & P. Smeyers (red.), *Opvoeding en onderwijs leren zien. Een inleiding in interpretatief onderzoek.* Amsterdam: Uitgeverij Boom, pp. 292-310.

Murray, C.D. & J. Sixsmith (2003). E-mail: A Qualitative Research Medium for Interviewing? In: N. Fielding, *Interviewing. Volume II. Sage Benchmarks in Social Research Methods.* London: Sage, pp. 128-148.

Ostrander, S.A. (2003, orig. 1993). 'Surely You're Not in this Just to be Helpful'. Access, Rapport, and Interviews in Three Studies of Elites. In: N. Fielding, *Interviewing. Volume III. Sage Benchmarks in Social Research Methods.* London: Sage, pp. 389-403.

Patton, M.Q. (1990). *Qualitative Evaluation and Research Methods.* Newbury Park: Sage.
Puchta, C. & J. Potter (2004). *Focus Group Practice.* London: Sage.

Royers, T. & L. de Ree (2003). De visuele prikkelmethode. *KWALON 23*, vol. 8, nr. 2, pp. 127-137.
Rubin, H. & I. Rubin (1995, 2005). *Qualitative Interviewing. The Art of Hearing Data.* Thousand Oaks: Sage.
Ruyter, K. de & N. Scholl (2001). *Kwalitatief marktonderzoek. Theorie en praktijkcases.* Den Haag: LEMMA.

Saldaña, Johnny (2009). *The Coding Manual for Qualitative Researchers.* London: Sage
Schensul, S.L., J.J. Schensul & M.D. LeCompte (1999). *Essential Ethnographic Methods. Observations, Interviews and Questionnaires.* Walnut Creek: Altamira Press, vol. 2 van de 'Ethnographer's Toolkit'.
Silverman (2006). *Interpreting Qualitative Data. Methods for Analyzing Talk, Text and Interaction.* London: Sage.
Smaling, A. (1987). *Methodologische objectiviteit en kwalitatief onderzoek.* Lisse: Swets en Zeitlinger.
Smaling, A. (1990). Objectiviteit en rolneming. In: I. Maso & A. Smaling (red.), *Objectiviteit in kwalitatief onderzoek.* Meppel: Boom, pp. 30-49.
Smaling, Adri (2003) Inductive, Analogical, and Communicative Generalization. *International Journal of QualitativeMethods*2(1).Zie http://www.ualberta.ca/ ‹iiqm/backissues/2_1/html/smaling.html
Smaling, A. (2007). The meaning of empathic understanding in human inquiry. In: A.-T. Tymieniecka (ed.), *Analecta Husserliana XCIV*, New York: Springer Verlag, pp. 309-341.
Stalpers, J. (2007). Elicitatietechnieken in kwalitatief onderzoek. *KWALON 34*, vol. 12, nr. 1, pp. 32-39.
Stroeken, H. (2000). *Kleine psychologie van het gesprek.* Amsterdam: Boom.

Temme, B. & A. Bikker (1999). *Leidraad groepsbijeenkomsten.* Den Haag: B&A Groep.

Vogel, H.P. & Th.M.M. Verhallen (1983). Technieken van kwalitatief onderzoek 2. *Tijdschrift voor Marketing,* January , pp. 28-33.
Vries, G. de (1995). *De ontwikkeling van wetenschap. Een inleiding in de wetenschapsfilosofie.* Groningen: Wolters-Noordhoff

Wester, F. & V. Peters (2004). *Kwalitatieve analyse. Uitgangspunten en procedures.* Bussum: Coutinho.
Whalley Hammell, K., Ch. Carpenter & I. Dyck (2002). *Using Qualitative Research. A Practical Introduction for Occupational and Physical Therapists.* Edinburgh: Churchill Livingstone.
Whyte, W.F. (2003). Interviewing for Organizational Research. In: N. Fielding, *Interview-ing. Volume I. Sage Benchmarks in Social Research Methods.* London: Sage, pp. 13-29.

Wolcott, H.F. (2005). *The Art of Fieldwork.* Walnut Creek: Altamira Press.

Zuckerman, H. (2003, orig. 1972). Interviewing an Ultra-Elite. In: N. Fielding, *Interviewing. Volume III. Sage Benchmarks in Social Research Methods.* London: Sage, pp. 373-388.

INDEX